MW00436285

THE WORDS

WE LEFT

BEHIND

CALLIE BYRNES

**THOUGHT
CATALOG**
Books

THOUGHTCATALOG.COM

THOUGHT CATALOG Books

Copyright © 2024 Callie Byrnes.

All rights reserved. No part of this book may be reproduced or transmitted in any form or any means, electronic or mechanical, without prior written consent and permission from Thought Catalog.

Published by Thought Catalog Books, an imprint of Thought Catalog, a digital magazine owned and operated by The Thought & Expression Co. Inc., an independent media organization founded in 2010 and based in the United States of America. For stocking inquiries, contact stockists@shopcatalog.com.

Produced by Chris Lavergne and Noelle Beams
Art direction and design by KJ Parish
Creative editorial direction by Brianna Wiest
Circulation management by Isidoros Karamitopoulos

thoughtcatalog.com | shopcatalog.com

First Edition, Limited Edition Pressing
Printed in the United States of America

ISBN 978-1-949759-81-5

To everyone who finds themselves
in the margins of this book:

Thank you. I love you. I'm sorry.

ACATALEPSY

(n.) real or apparent impossibility of arriving
at certain knowledge or full comprehension

————

WE STAND SIDE-BY-SIDE on a clear night, so close that if I were to reach out, my knuckles would graze yours. I try to connect the stars with my line of sight while you paint pictures with the smoke that drifts from your long, thin fingers.

I tell you about how I wanted to be an astronomer once, how I used to stargaze from my grandmother's countryside patio and draw the sky on the back of receipts. I tell you about my family. I tell you that sometimes I can't make sense of the world no matter how hard I try, that my thoughts don't seem to connect and neither does anything else in life. Sometimes I feel as disjointed as every pinpoint in the night sky.

But then there is you, with your cigarette lips that smile ever so slightly when I speak, with your eyes that follow my line of thought like it's the red string that will lead us out of this maze. You make me feel less alone in all this empty atmosphere because I am used to being lost in my thoughts, but you remind me what it's like to be found.

"Why astronomy?" you ask, long after I've forgotten what I was saying.

I tug at the hem of my dress and shrug, suddenly shy, as if I've been ousted from the darkness, no longer able to hide behind the night. Your attention has always been a spotlight I crave until it leaves me feeling exposed.

"Because I want to understand it," I say eventually.

Because I want to understand the vastness of it all, or maybe just my smallness. Because I want to understand if there are dead ends or if there are some things that really exist in forevers. Because I want to understand the things that have existed long before me and that will continue long after me, too. But maybe what I really mean is that I want to understand my place in it all—or maybe just that I want it all to understand me.

I can tell from the tilt of your smile that you've already anticipated the words on the tip of my tongue, connecting the dots of my thoughts effortlessly, and it's only then that I finally understand why I stopped looking for answers in the stars.

ADUMBRATE

(v.) to foreshadow vaguely

———

THE MAZE OF THE MUSEUM has become the backdrop of this budding friendship, though none of the paintings interest me quite like you do. We pause to read the placards on the wall, but really we are reading each other—our reactions, the details we linger on and those we choose to leave behind. We tell our stories in the context of the art surrounding us.

Our lives have been colored in so differently, but here we start to see the bigger picture: the still life of a fruit bowl becomes the thick Midwestern summers spent eating wild strawberries straight from the vine with my father. The painting of Mary holding baby Jesus becomes the walls of the church where you spent every Sunday morning growing up, the one that taught you about faith. Under the bright fluorescent lighting, we admire every brushstroke of the past that we paint for the other.

Halfway through the exhibits, we step out into the garden for a break and find a bench that allows us to sit, turned, face-to-face. You tell me about how it's beautiful here but sometimes you still miss your hometown, so I ask, "Why did your family decide to move, anyway?"

You look up at the foamy clouds floating above us as if you'll find the reason hidden somewhere in the steam. "In those last few months there, we were all really struggling," you admit. "My mom prayed about it a lot. One day, when she was mowing the lawn, she said to God, 'If you show me three white feathers by the time I'm done, I'll know it's a sign.'"

I wait for you to continue the story, but you just stare up at the sky, content. "And?" I prompt.

You grin wryly, though I'm not entirely sure it's meant for me. "She found three exactly, and we started packing the next day. Now every time I see a white feather, I know I'm on the right path."

My first reaction is to wonder why anyone would let something so small impact such a big decision, because I may count on flower petals and make wishes on the numbers on the clock, but I've never believed in anything strongly enough to imagine such an act of faith—not a deity, not a theory, not even myself. I want to ask you if you ever questioned it, if there was ever even an inkling of doubt that seeped in, but

I already see the answer in your smile.

"Let's go back inside," you say suddenly, hoisting yourself onto your feet and holding out a hand to help me to my own. "I want to see what else is here."

As we approach the doors leading back into the museum, you come to a sudden halt. I look at you, confused, then follow your line of sight to the cement path before us, where one small white feather rests on the threshold.

"See?" you say, your eyes crinkling in the corners as they meet the surprise in mine. "We're exactly where we're meant to be."

And there is something in your conviction that makes me believe it, too.

ALBATROSS

(n.) something that causes persistent
deep concern or anxiety; something that
greatly hinders accomplishment

———

THE FIRST TIME I SAW YOU after you broke
my heart, I was with the boy who made me laugh the
way you did. We were getting ice cream at the parlor
you promised we'd try that he now brought me to all
the time. We were standing in line, pointing out our
favorite flavors through the freezer window, when
I noticed you sitting on a bench from the corner of
my eye. I spent the whole hour trying not to look
toward the edge of the room you haunted because,
in the early days of mourning you, the only way I
knew how to handle the grief was to not acknowl-
edge it at all.

The second time I saw you after you broke my
heart, I was with the boy whose words upended me
because they were the exact ones you'd said to me
first. I always tried to discount the similarities, tell-
ing myself that even stuck in this cycle, I could find
a way to make it all work, but then I walked into

that coffee shop years after we'd both moved away from it and there you were. Though I sat with him on the other side of the room, my eyes kept drifting over to you, if only because I couldn't believe the odds that in trying to escape my past, I once again found myself barreling right back toward it. When we finally left, letting the glass door shut definitively behind us, I told myself I wouldn't look back.

The last time I saw you after you broke my heart, I was with the boy whose openness reminded me of why I'd once been so drawn to you. Maybe that's why I found it so hard to trust him. I never could figure out what was more terrifying: the thought of keeping myself so closed off to the possibilities that I missed them completely or the idea of opening myself up to them, only to realize I'd never quite escaped the labyrinth I entered the day I met you. After months of holding myself back, I was finally ready to let him in, but then I looked up to see you standing a few yards in front of us, your silhouette a stop sign that halted me in my tracks. As I watched you disappear around the corner, I felt a tug on all those stitches that held me together, as if you'd plucked the end of the string and pulled it along with you, leaving me to unravel.

There's a cruelty to our fate, I realize now—because I am destined to lose you, I am destined to be lost, two flight risks doomed from the jump. After all this time, I still can't quite figure out whether you're a warning or a red herring, the sign from the universe telling me to leave or the manifestation of that part of me that's terrified to stay. Sometimes I fear that in trying to break this pattern, I have only cursed myself to relive it, waiting for the day I'll see you again to remind me that even when I've moved on from you, a part of you will never move on from me.

AQUIVER

(adj.) marked by trembling or quivering

––––––––

I CANNOT EXPLAIN the electric currents that run between us, but the look in your eyes when they meet mine is a shock to my system, the strike that makes my breath catch. I cannot explain why your touch scorches every particle of flesh it grazes, how every time you exhale against my skin you create constellations of goosebumps down my neck, a map of all the unmarred terrain just aching to ignite. I cannot explain the feeling that reverberates through my ribcage at our moment of impact, the seismic force that makes every atom in my body stutter and shake and shiver—all I know is that to be loved by you is to be destroyed by you.

ARCANE

(adj.) known or knowable only to
a few people; mysterious

———

I'M TOLD I FEEL LOST because I'm a Pisces, and I start to wonder if everyone born in the days around me feels as unmoored as I've become. I teach myself to read natal charts, trying to pinpoint exactly where this all began. I look for answers in search engines: If Mercury was in retrograde when I was born, will it always feel like everything is going wrong? If most of my planets are in the twelfth house, am I destined to come undone? I keep waiting for the stars to align, for the planets to finally ingress, for all of this to someday make sense.

In the meantime, I start learning about palmistry, try to interpret the breaks in my wrinkles. But in certain light, my fate line is unreadable, and my love line never explains why I sometimes feel so unlovable, and if my skin knows something I don't, it prefers to keep its secrets. It has become the embodiment of all the things I can't understand about myself.

"You should start looking into your subconscious," a friend tells me, but the dream dictionary never explains why my every nightmare is about someone I haven't spoken to in years. I waste away the hours of the night trying to explain myself in circles as if somehow it might unburden me from the weight of everyone's disapproval. Even in my sleep, I keep fighting these old battles, reliving cycles I know will never change, but I'm always left heartbroken by it anyway.

And in the morning, when I wake up sweating, I pull tarot card after tarot card, hoping I'll find a prophecy somewhere in the pictures, a promise this will all turn out alright. But no matter how many I draw, they always answer like a Magic 8 Ball: reply hazy, cannot predict, ask again, ask again, ask again.

ASKEW

(adj.) out of line; at an angle

————

IT'S MY BIRTHDAY, and I'm searching through all the people who showed up at the bar to celebrate me in hopes of finding someone who might actually see me. Everyone is laughing and I am breaking, and I can't seem to figure out how anyone can so much as smile on a day like this. Because it's my birthday, and nothing in the world feels right anymore, and I desperately need to believe somebody else notices it, too.

I find you at one of the tables, talking to a few of our friends who watch in confusion as I wrap my fingers around your forearm and ask, "Can I talk to you, please?"

"Of course," you say, trying to sound casual, but I see the concern in your eyes as you finish your beer and follow me to the other side of the room. It's only when we find a table that's turned away from everyone we know that I can breathe again.

"What's wrong?" you ask, sitting down in the chair across from me.

I'm not sure how I'm supposed to answer that. Because this room is full of people who orchestrated this outing, a surprise just for me, and they have done everything they can to ensure I don't have to spend even a minute alone. And it seems like my life is finally taking shape, like I'm heading in the right direction, because everyone tells me they're so proud of me and that I should be, too. Most days, it feels like the stars are aligning, and even I'm surprised by all these little strokes of luck, these puzzle pieces that fall into place almost effortlessly. The ground beneath me feels steady in a way it never has before, yet somehow it has taken everything in me to keep myself upright because my feet can't seem to stop slipping out from under the weight of everything. I don't know how to tell you that it's crushing me.

But when I open my mouth, I burst out crying, any possible explanation drowned out. Because my favorite song is playing over the loudspeaker, and someone is calling from across the bar to ask if they can buy me a drink, and if I could catch my breath for long enough to tell you anything, I would have to admit that maybe the only thing wrong here is me.

AURORA

(n.) dawn

———

MORNING DEW GLISTENS green along the side of the road as I drive, bleary-eyed, toward a sky that turns from a dusky gray to a blinding, trembling orange. Headlights sparkle in the distance like fireflies flitting in the underbrush, and I wonder if I look like that across the stretch of highway, too, just a blip of light in the distance lost beneath the glow. I wish I could paint the purples into the creases of sky, wish I could cut fabrics from the fragments of morning and wrap them tightly around me. I feel magic in these moments, awe swelling deep inside my chest, and for the first time in a long time, my smallness no longer scares me. There is a certain serenity in the succumbing, in becoming a single brush stroke of something truly divine.

BELEAGUER

(v.) to trouble

———

I WISH I'D NEVER met someone who altered the way I think. But I did change, and then you left, and now no one recognizes me.

BEWITCH

(v.) to cast a spell over

————

IT IS A GENERATIONAL blessing, to know what it takes to be loved.

I have inherited my mother's laugh, the way it can shimmer through a crowded room, its luster reflecting the attention back to me. I have learned it's not about batting your eyelashes or twirling your hair, merely mirroring—this ability to look at someone and see them for who they are, then becoming exactly what they want you to be. I meticulously mimic those facets you value most—your opinions, your disposition, your idiosyncrasies—until you're lulled into a steady ease. Basking in my disco ball glow, you can't convince yourself to leave.

It is easier than I thought it would be, becoming this shiny object, this coveted thing. It is an empowering feeling, knowing I can make myself into something so valuable you can't afford to lose me. And I am loved, I am loved, I am loved—exactly what I've always wanted to be.

BOMBINATE

(v.) buzz

———

THIS TOWN HAS ALWAYS been too small for me, but sometimes there are moments when I feel like I might belong. Like when we're sitting out in the fields at twilight under a sky like layers of frothy frosting and the humidity sticks to my skin in sheets. When fireflies blink around our heads in indiscernible patterns and cicadas sing us familiar songs and the air tastes like the electricity of oncoming storms, and it's all so beautiful that I don't even care that the overgrown grass scratches at the backs of my knees. Everything is humming in sync—the sky and the earth, you and me—as if it all has come full circle, and it's here, and it's now, and it's us. Maybe I am still a Kansas girl at heart because I will always dream of Oz but these ruby slippers only find their home in pure Midwestern soil.

BRONTIDE

(n.) a low muffled sound like distant thunder

———

KNOWLEDGE IS POWER, they say, but it makes me weak in the knees. I am always the one who knows all the things I'd rather not, the pieces of information that suffocate the soul and crush the heart. I am the bearer of bad news, the messenger you shoot when you realize I knew, god, I always knew. I just didn't know how to tell you.

Knowledge is power, they say, until suddenly it's not. Most days, I miss the bliss of ignorance, of never having to ask whether it's better to speak or to die because it's all beginning to feel the same. The leadup to the truth is like the calm before the storm, and it makes everything inside me tremble like the growls that shake these paper walls mere minutes before lightning strikes and both of our hearts stop.

CADENCE

(n.) a falling inflection of the voice

———

I STILL FIND YOU in the way I speak, in those little turns of phrase I got to know so intimately. I like to pronounce certain words the way you once did just to make me laugh, though no one else seems to understand why; only I know every smile it brings to my lips belongs, at least in part, to you. Even my speech patterns still mimic the rhythm of your heart-beat because sometimes the people who enter your life unexpectedly are the ones who change it irrevo-cably, and in these tiny, integral ways, you have left your mark on me. You, whose words slowed when we were alone; you, whose voice cradled my name as if it were the most beautiful thing in the world, so convincing I had no choice but to believe it. I mourn the day when I forget the sound of you because it'll be more than just proof that you're gone—it'll be the realization that part of me is, too.

CATACLYSM

(n.) catastrophe

———

YOU SHUFFLE THE CARDS carefully, wait until one falls onto the table before you flip it over and smile. "The Lovers," you say, sliding it toward me. But when you pull the next few, the quirk of your mouth begins to falter. "You have this need for independence that wars with the romantic in you," you tell me. "For some reason, you struggle to open your heart."

How can I not? I can't help but think. Every time I've left the doorway wide open, something has always come along to slam it shut. The only kind of love I've ever known has been the peace in the eye of a hurricane, the final breath as the flood drags me under, the lightning strike that burns my whole world to the ground—that one moment of ecstasy that cannot exist without catastrophe. The only kind of love I've ever known is natural disaster.

I want to believe there's something different out there. I want to believe there are people who can make a home of someone without knocking all the foundations down. Sometimes I'm terrified I wouldn't recognize love if it didn't match my scars because I can't convince myself it's real if it never leaves a mark. Most days, I'd rather lock all the doors and board the windows shut, because even if these hollow rooms feel lonely, at least I'll know I'm better off.

CHIAROSCURO

(n.) pictorial representation in terms of
light and shade without regard to color

———————

THEY CHOOSE A ROOM with floor-to-ceiling
windows for your funeral, discounting the fact that
these short November days rarely bother to hold
space for the light. By the time we file into the harsh
fluorescent glare of the memorial service, it's already
pitch black outside; instead of overlooking this town
you had once called home, the darkened panes of
glass have become reflective, a murky funhouse mir-
ror we're all forced to face for the rest of the night.

It seems fitting, almost funny, in a cruel, twisted
way, how the darkness that once followed you seems
to follow us even here, and now we can't ignore
the way it has altered our reality. In losing you to
yourself, we have lost something else: our innocence,
maybe, or the idea that we ever had it to begin with.
Because looking back, I start to see the shadows
clearly, those charcoal smudges along the edge of
every picture-perfect moment. It was in your silence
during dinner, it was in the way you retreated when

we showed up to your home, it was carved into the gauntness of your face the last time I saw you. It was in the way you didn't even say goodbye, you just disappeared.

Now it seems to be everywhere around me: in the words your husband speaks from the podium, in the way your father's shoulders shake, in our haunted expressions etched into the pane of glass. I see it in myself, too, how it's made a home inside my chest, wrapping its bony fingers around my neck. I still can't figure out if it crept in after that morning I woke up to the news of your death or if it's been there for a long time and you just finally made me notice it.

I wonder if this is how it'll always be, if every memory we look back on will feel a little less happy, if every good day going forward will hold an added dimension, a stark contrast to what we know lies under the surface. All I know is that I'm sitting here at your funeral, staring into the mirror of the window, our first glimpse of this new world without you. The longer I watch my reflection, the less certain I become about whether I'm the girl under the blinding lights or the one who stares back at me from the glass, overlayed by this unrelenting night. Maybe the truth is that I'm both, because when one of us moves, so does the other, and I'm not convinced that will change even after I leave this godforsaken room.

CHIMERICAL

(adj.) existing only as the product
of unchecked imagination

———

"I WISH I'D KNOWN you when we were younger," you tell me on one of those rare nights when the darkness creeping in from the window unveils all our vulnerabilities. "I think it would've made everything so much easier."

In these quiet moments between us, when we have nothing left to hide from one another, it's easy to imagine a world where we met in the schoolyard on a sunny adolescent afternoon. "You're gonna get dirty," you'd tell me when you notice me lying in the grass, and I'd squint up at you skeptically, unsure if this is your attempt at comradery or if you're just another boy who pulls pigtails for fun. But you'd extend an olive branch by sitting down beside me, unfazed by the new stains on your jeans, so I'd show you how to comb through the weeds with your fingers patiently in search of four-leaf clovers. When I'd find one, I'd pluck it tenderly from the earth and offer this good luck charm to you; you'd go home in the afternoon and store it in your desk drawer, where you would leave it to live for years.

In this timeline, I'd be sitting on your mother's living room couch when you discover your favorite TV show, the one that in another life you'd tell me about in hindsight. We'd spend our free time analyzing the newest episodes and contemplating in hypotheticals, and I'd never admit that I only watch because I can't help but love anything that makes your eyes shine. I'd find new ways to bring it up, keep formulating new questions to ask, even if they aren't really relevant, even if I don't really care to know the answers, only because I care about what you think about anything and everything.

In this version of the world, I'd be there to hold your hand during your first heartbreak. I'd be there to stand beside you at the funeral and to pretend I don't notice you crying on the drive back home. I'd be there to hold you back when the world makes you so bitter that all you want to do is fight, but even when I couldn't, I'd be there just in time to wipe away the blood, to bandage your fists, to draw little Sharpie hearts inside the bruises on your knees, because maybe when you'd see them, it would somehow ease the ache.

And in this parallel universe, where everything could be different but where we are the same, I wonder if you'd still forget my birthday. I wonder if I'd still stay up all night staring at the blank screen of my phone, just waiting for your call. I wonder if you'd still choose her over me and if I'd still choose you over everything. In this world where I met you sooner and loved you longer, I wonder if anything really changes at all.

CIRCUMSTANTIAL

(adj.) marked by careful attention to detail

———

I HATE THE SKEPTIC you've made of me, how I can no longer leave a stone unturned between us. I can't prove that you're lying, but I can prove you've changed the way you speak, how you've begun to condense paragraphs into single lines and single lines into silence. You can tell me nothing is wrong, but my name on your tongue tastes differently—you used to draw out every syllable like you never wanted them to end, but now the letters are stilted, clipped, as if you'd like nothing more than to purge yourself of me. And in those moments where our eyes meet, there's a vacancy in your stare, as if you've given up on finding what you once saw in me, as if there's nothing you recognize there. You can blame your job, you can blame your mom, you can blame the weekdays or the weather or the news, but that doesn't explain how even your best days have begun to feel like our worst, because every piece of you they bring back just reminds me of what we have left to lose. You can call me anxious, you can call me crazy, but it's better than playing your fool. When you tell me we're okay, I want to believe you—it just wouldn't be the truth.

CLANDESTINE

(adj.) marked by, held in, or
conducted with secrecy

———

I WANT TO SCREAM IT from the rooftops—
this *I love you I love you I love you*—but I can't even
bring myself to whisper it in the dark. Instead, I tap
out the message in Morse code against the inside
of your wrist, captivated by the way your pulse an-
swers. I ignore the ache of knowing this is the only
way you'll ever say it back.

And there's nothing for us to get away with here,
but that doesn't stop us from trying. Every moment
between us feels stolen. From what? I want to ask
you. From who? I'm not sure why we have to pry our
time from the cold, dead hands of the clock like it's a
criminal offense. I'm not sure why we hide every trace
of each other like it's some sort of damning evidence.

But I'll keep telling people the spare key in my
wallet is my own. And you'll keep telling all your
friends that you're going home alone. And we'll
keep pretending that in keeping this secret, we're

keeping it sacred, though our words have begun to feel like blasphemy. In these sacrosanct days, I'm holding on to blind faith in a gospel I'm no longer sure I believe.

COMESTIBLE

(n.) food

————

YOU'RE GRIEVING in the kitchen and I want to tell you that I love you, but instead I crack an egg into a bowl. You are hurting and I am stirring in the flour, hoping the culmination of these small actions will help ease the ache. I add a heaping cup of sugar, unlike the half I usually do, because after years of being taught that to love yourself is to deny yourself, I can't bear to apply that principle to you.

As I spoon the dough onto the baking sheet, diligently making sure each dollop is two inches apart, all I can think about is the moment it will meet your lips, surrendering its sweetness. I want to give you everything you cannot give yourself, the things I can't even stomach for myself—this sweet-tooth compassion, this confectionary mercy. To love you is to nourish you.

CORUSCATE

(v.) to flash or reflect light in bright beams; sparkle

———

YOU SIT IN the driver's seat, tired and grumpy and itching to get home. I sit beside you, staring out the window, uncharacteristically at ease in this new situation. It has been a long time since I sat in a silence so comfortable, so natural, and I can't help but bask in it. Somehow, this small Ford Explorer feels like home.

"Idiot," you mumble to a driver on your left, but I hardly notice. Instead, something else has caught my attention—the gray December street lined with glimmering lights, sparkling and blinking into designs so dazzling I can't tear my eyes away. I turn my head to watch as they pass.

You shake your head, hardly giving them a second glance before they're gone. "That's distracting."

I smile. "All beautiful things are."

And when I turn back to you, you aren't paying

attention to the road anymore. Instead, you're look-ing at me with an expression I haven't seen in a long time.

CRESCENDO

(n.) a gradual increase in volume
of a musical passage

————

WHEN THE STORM BEGINS, you find me next to the sliding door, watching the raindrops streak across the glass. The world beyond it has become blurred like the murky center of a crystal ball; you know me well enough to understand my silence is less meditative than anxious, that in the gloom, I see a doomsday yet to be foretold.

"It's just a little rain," you tell me, but doesn't it always start that way? Every disaster begins with a miracle; everything that brings life can take it away. For some reason, I cannot imagine the end of a drought that doesn't become the flood that drowns me.

You sigh and sit down next to me on the linoleum floor, letting your arm become a shelter around my shoulders. "Close your eyes," you command.

I listen because it's you, or maybe because it's the only

thing to do. Even the darkness behind my eyelids is less daunting than the weather, but only just.

"Now listen to the sound of the rain on the roof," you say. "Isn't it pretty?"

I guess it is, in a way, though I've never thought about it before. The beat is almost soothing when isolated from the rest.

Then your voice: "Pretend it's the drummers in a marching band. Can you see the parade?"

I scrunch my brow, press my eyelids even tighter together. If I try hard enough, the image starts to take shape—blue coats flapping in the wind, heels clicking against the street to the rhythm of the raindrops. I'm somewhere on the sidelines, watching them pass, when a sudden rumble of thunder throws me out of my reverie and back onto the kitchen floor.

"Shh," you whisper, tightening your arm around me. "That's just the music."

When I close my eyes again, I realize you're right— the musicians have begun their song, their drumsticks skittering across the surface of the snares. It starts out slow, meandering, but the sound begins to build, the bass thumping against my ribcage. I hear a chiming sound and look over to see someone is playing a triangle, the beater clanging against all three steel edges. When I notice the flashes of gold in the distance, I know it's just the sun's reflection off the cymbals in that split second when they come crashing together, the metallic clatter bringing the concert to its climax.

As the band marches away, you're still beside me, your arm on my shoulders as steady as my heartbeat when you say, "See? The world is here to make music for you."

CYNOSURE

(n.) a center of attraction or attention; North Star

————

I HATE THE WAY we're pulled toward each other, two separate currents that come crashing together. Like we're compasses frantically spinning our needles round and round, desperate to find a new direction, but the magnetic field between us always points due North. No matter what we do, we always find our way back to square one.

And I wish I could love someone the way I loved you. I wish that when I was with him, my eyes wouldn't wander to yours, and I wish that every time I tried to run away, I didn't end up at your door. I wish spending time with other people didn't remind me how much lonelier I am without you. I wish that when he touched me, I didn't forget who his fingers belonged to.

I can deny it, and I can resist it, but I can't hide from the truth: no matter where life leads me, I always come back to you.

DALLIANCE

(n.) a brief, playful love affair

———

I'M IN FLORENCE, the cultural mecca of the Western world, walking through thin, twisting passageways lined with buildings bursting with life. I imagine walking the same paths the artists did, my footsteps aligning like stars with the poets' on streets forged from centuries of dust. I wonder if this is how Dante felt when his eyes fell upon Beatrice for the first—no, second—time, if this is why Petrarch wrote poem after poem about his beloved Laura. Is this what makes the soul sigh?

I meet you on the steps in front of the church that looms overhead like God himself. You smile when you see me. I didn't know if I should meet you—I don't know you—but somehow, you convinced me to step out of my comfort zone and into your presence. You leave the next day on an early morning flight and you don't want to sleep. You want to feel the life of the city one more time. You don't want to be alone. Sometimes, here, I feel so alone.

You hold out your hand. I take it.

We walk from bar to bar, to places I've never seen despite living here long enough. I drink a margarita that makes the darkened streets spin. They always seem to make them stronger here. The alcohol and the atmosphere make me bold, but when your questions become too personal, I hesitate; you laugh.

"Why are you so afraid?" you ask. "We're perfect strangers. There's no one better to tell."

You're right—I know you are—but my confessions catch in my throat. I don't want you to know me yet.

We leave behind our empty glasses in search of something new. My fingers skim along the aging buildings as I float down the sidewalk weightlessly, like every string of gravity is falling away from me. You pull me back onto solid ground and set me down on a stone railing. You move closer. Your gaze wanders down to my smile; your mouth is quick to follow. I feel your lips, soft, slow.

I know I should leave, but I'm so entranced by you that every time I pull away, your gaze pulls me back. I think maybe I'll regret this. I think maybe I never will.

The sun peeks up behind the city in a heavenly glow, and every now and then people emerge from dusky homes. It feels too early still. Every time you hear a sound, you pull me tightly against your chest, shielding me from the view of sleep-glazed eyes. Our breathing is heavy, rough; I can feel your heartbeat colliding with mine.

When we part ways in the morning, you lace our fingers together until we find the fork in the road where our paths diverge.

"Hopefully we'll meet again," you say with a half-moon smile. I know we won't. We're only meant to be a single knot in our threads of fate; but though Dante met Beatrice no more than twice, they live forever in his poetry—immortalized.

DENOUEMENT

(n.) the outcome of a complex sequence of events

———

THE END OF YOUR existence meant unraveling the decades and packing them into boxes, and I can't help but wonder how a life built so diligently can be dismantled in just a matter of days. Now somehow, all your favorite things become junk at the bottom of our drawers, distant reminders of the things you must've loved so fiercely once if only we dig deep enough to remember. When I stand in the wreckage of it all, alone in the bare bones of your old home, I swear if I listen closely enough, I can hear your old record player still turning somewhere, searching for the music that once filled every corner of the room but only finding the static at the end of the vinyl—until, with one final click of the door shut behind me, I'm only left with silence.

DESUETUDE

(n.) disuse

———

WHEN I FIND a box of your old clothes in the basement, I have no choice but to try them on. I can tell by their design that they haven't been worn in years, that they are a relic of a past you, one I've never met before. I think about my own wardrobe, how sometimes I'll look at a silky dress dangling innocently from a hanger and the fabric of time will collapse around me and I'll be standing somewhere else, watching a younger me running through a sprinkler or dancing on a street corner or getting my heart broken for the very first time. There are so many stories woven into the threads of what we wear, and as I pull one of your shirts over my head, I wonder what slice of your life I am stepping into, what parts of the world it has seen. Did it ever witness how hard you love? The abandon of your laugh? Those ever-churning waters of your grief? I wonder if by wearing it, I am allowing you to give those parts of yourself to me.

I watch myself transform in the mirror above the dresser, how even my face seems to take on certain attributes I've only ever associated with you. Is this the key to holding on to the people we miss the most? In remembering you—the way you dressed, the way you talked, the way you moved—I become you. On the days you feel most distant, I can return to this box in the basement and hold these instants of your life in my hands; I can mold them to my form, and when I look in the mirror, I will find you.

DIAPHANOUS

(adj.) characterized by such fineness of
texture as to permit seeing through

———

YOU SET THE MUG DOWN in front of me on
the kitchen table and all it takes is one sip of the
coffee to feel as though you've ripped the skin right
from my bones. You've made it exactly how I like,
though I don't remember ever teaching you. How
could I forget when every moment spent with you
stays seared into my psyche? There are no words I've
ever given you that don't rattle around inside me
somewhere.

How is it that you've come to know me so well with-
out me even noticing? While I've been preoccupied
with identifying every seam of your selfhood, have
you been standing across from me this whole time,
doing the same? I wonder if you, too, keep a catalog
of every fold of my brain, always waiting for the day
you'll get to use it.

This realization makes me feel fragile, like it would
only take one cast stone for this all to come tumbling

down. I have spent decades building up these walls, only to realize they're made of glass. I never recognized how badly I wanted to be seen until you looked right through me.

DUENDE

(n.) a higher state of emotion or
inspiration in response to art

———

WE ARE MENACES TO the museum-goers,
hardly able to stifle our laughter behind our hands
as we slip from room to room. Nearly every paint-
ing has a quirk we can exploit for our own amuse-
ment, and while others quietly appreciate the art
surrounding us, we weave it into our inside jokes,
making a mockery of masterpieces. Every exhibit
looks so much more colorful when I'm with you.

But as we near the center of the museum, your
demeanor transforms, a solemnity settling into
your smile. It's only then that I realize you've been
leading me down a pathway you seem to know by
heart, a route that leads us away from the crowds
of people and to a corridor where the walls are
painted a pristine white. You stop just outside a
solid wooden door.

"Ready?" you ask, suddenly serious, as if we haven't
run around all afternoon breaking rules and ducking

out of sight whenever the security guard rounded the corner.

I nod, any attempt at humor dying in the back of my throat. I'm not sure what I'm supposed to be ready for or how to prepare myself, but there seems to be no other right answer than to jump in blindly with you.

I follow you into the room, and when the door shuts, I'm overcome by the immensity of the darkness, as if we've been cut off from the rest of the world, left to drift out into the void. But when my eyes adjust, I notice a small pyramid in the corner of the room, undulating a brilliant blue.

"It's coming from up there," you explain, pointing to the ceiling. "See? It's all a projection."

You're right—the apparent object is a reflection of light so simple its execution perplexes me. In the emptiness that surrounds us, it seems to grow without ever moving, taking up all the space in the room.

"Amazing, isn't it?" you ask, and I realize then how intently you're gazing at it, as if the answers to the universe are somewhere buried in the blue, waiting to reveal themselves to you. "I come in here every week just to see it."

It's not the sort of admission I'd expect from you—it's too sincere, too earnest, too revealing in a way you'd usually resist because you only seem to love attention when you still have somewhere to hide. But in this room, you are a wide-eyed child entranced by a trick of light, too preoccupied with your wonder to pretend to be anything else. For a few moments, neither of us moves, each in awe of a simple masterpiece: you admire the triangle, and I, you.

DULCET

(adj.) pleasing to the ear

———

SOMETIMES, AFTER YOU think I've already fallen asleep, I hear the soft murmur of your voice creeping up from under the rush of the running faucet, your tongue tasting the wrong notes and broken lyrics of your favorite songs; it always makes me smile. I've never told you this before because I know it would embarrass you, that you'd think twice before ever singing to yourself so carelessly again. You wouldn't believe all these little mistakes you mouth in the middle of the night compose the sweetest lullaby I've ever heard.

EFFERVESCENCE

(n.) forming bubbles; an appealingly lively quality

———

WE'RE TWO BOTTLES of prosecco deep and swimming through the late-night humidity, but it's easy to keep my head afloat when the alcohol has left me weightless. Nothing could sink this sparkling feeling, the euphoria of being drunk in a city where no one knows my name—no one, that is, but you. You grab me by the hand and spin me through the streets.

When we pass by the doorway of a club, the blaring bass rattling the windows from the inside out, you pull us into the entrance of a room that is somehow darker than the night itself. The world falls away from me—my surroundings, your face, the floor, everything but the music hammering against my ribcage and your fingers tight around my own. The wine buzzes through every inch of my body as I sway from room to room, no longer fully in control of myself.

I'm not sure how it happens: One minute, we are traipsing through a sea of strangers, but the next, we are standing on top of a trembling speaker, vibrating with the music as we stare down at the crowd. From above the writhing figures, I don't feel human—I am just a faraway presence, the fly on the wall, the god in the steeple. When your hands find my waist, I'm brought back into my body; I squeal as you lift me off the ground.

"Grab on to the balcony," you instruct me, and it's only then that I look up to see one suspended above us. When you hoist me up, gravity seems to extract its leaden fingers from around me, allowing me to float upwards until my hands wrap around the railing. I pull myself over, joining the ranks of people flitting in and out of the room; suddenly, you're there with me, too.

"Are we supposed to be here?" I ask.

You grin back in response. "No."

My brain tells me this is a bad idea, that I should climb back down the way we came, but my body bows backward in laughter. You catch me before I lose my balance, as if I had any to begin with, because whatever has been keeping me upright all night surely isn't me. You twirl me around the balcony until we are dancing on nothing but air.

I am stopped in my tracks by another pair of hands, this one rougher than your own. "That's enough of that," I hear someone say, and I look up to see the security guard lifting me away from you, carrying me toward the exit. I reach toward you and find your fingers already grasping for mine.

The security guard discards us onto the pavement of the alleyway outside the club, yelling that we shouldn't bother trying to get back in, but even as he slams the door behind us, I can't stop laughing. The prosecco has loosened something in me, fizzling away all my inhibitions and stripping the city of its limits. I know I'd already be halfway gone to the moon if you weren't still standing beside me, your hand anchoring me to the earth with a silent promise: where you go, I go.

EFFLORESCENCE

(n.) the action or process of developing and unfolding as if coming into flower; blossoming

————

WHEN YOU LOOK at me like that, I feel the flowers start to bloom. The cavity of my chest, once an arid wasteland, flourishes in the waves of your unremitting warmth. I've never known a green thumb that could coax these reluctant seeds to take root, but now there are roses wrapped around my ribcage, peonies clotting in my lungs, and somehow even the most difficult breath to take is sweeter than before. There are people who only covet beauty, who cannot appreciate a lovely thing without wanting to wrench it from the earth, but then there is you: you who cultivates so carefully, you who knows how to let a good thing grow. Even the rainfall doesn't scare me anymore, not when I know it isn't here to drown out what they want to weed from me. Only you understand that to love me is to handle me with care.

ELEGY

(n.) a song or poem expressing sorrow or lamentation especially for one who is dead

———

IT'S TEN IN the morning and the funeral has started, but I'm a hundred miles from the cemetery. I can't convince myself to pull that black gauzy dress from my closet, can't find the will to pull it over my head. I don't know how to stand in a crowd full of strangers and mourn you, not when I spent years learning how to lose you long before you died. I can't convince myself to do it anymore.

Because I said goodbye to you the last time we argued. I said goodbye to you the last time you called. I said goodbye to you on your hospital bed when they told me you were already gone. I said goodbye when I found the scarf you gave me four Christmases ago and again when I drove by your favorite shop last week. I've said goodbye so many times that I've grown sick of it.

But then someone will say something in just the same way that you once did and there you are again, except it's fifteen years ago and I'm sitting at the breakfast bar at your lake house. You're dancing around the kitchen while you make us ice cream sundaes, serenading me with a song I've never heard before, and I think it might be the most beautiful thing I've ever heard until you laugh, head thrown back, mouth wide open, and the sound usurps it immediately. It's the kind of moment I never want to lose, but before I can grab on to it, it's already gone. It always leaves an emptiness inside me, the glaring lack of something I didn't notice before.

Sometimes I wonder if I've been grieving the wrong things because you were always so much more than a person to me. You were peaceful mornings where the dawn shimmered across the waves and the whole world went quiet, still. You were long drives in a red convertible with the top down, the deep blue of the sky above us; you were the wind kissing my face, caressing my hair. You were the exhilaration of jumping headfirst into the water, and you were the stolen taste of pumpkin pie before dinner, and you were the sleepy intoxication of a third glass of wine. You were the reminder that nothing lasts forever, that sometimes you lose things before you even realize they're gone, and it all somehow makes what you once had so precious. I don't know if I'll ever be ready to say goodbye to that.

Maybe that's why, as the funeral ends and I finally convince myself to step outside, the first thing I do is look up at the sunlight seeping through a crevasse in the clouds. One hundred miles from here, the world is saying its goodbyes to you, but lost in the morning's opalescent glow, I can't stop myself from saying hello.

ELIXIR

(n.) a medicinal concoction

———

MILK BUBBLES UP along the edges of the pan like it's my own personal healing spring. The carton warns of yesterday's expiration date, but beggars can't be choosers, and I'm praying for a miracle here. The internet says it's the tryptophan that will make you tired, or maybe it's the peptides, or maybe it's just the placebo effect—I don't really care which is true. My anxiety has kept me awake for two weeks and I'm desperate to find anything that will put my nerves at ease.

I found a recipe with a promising description—"This will calm your mind to help your body sleep"—and I was so eager to see if it'd work that I didn't bother checking the ingredients before I began. I don't have cherry juice, but I do have a half-eaten carton of strawberries, and if I put them in the blender, it looks the same. The whir of the blades against the fleshy fruit reminds me of my brain, the way it never seems to stop grinding, as if there's a cog out of place. My mind feels as thick and formless as the puree.

I add the red liquid into the pan, watch as its contents mix and settle on a soothing pink. The same color as my backpack, ironically, the one that hangs on a hook in my room exactly parallel to my bed so that when I lie awake at night, my resistant eyes peeled open, I find myself staring at it for hours on end. I feel the sudden urge to leave the stove behind for just long enough to run down the stairs and through my bedroom door, unhook the bag from the wall, and throw it somewhere else—the closet, the floor, anywhere, as long as I don't have to spend another night memorizing its every seam.

But no—honey, I need honey. I pillage the cabinet above the counter until I find a bottle, the nectar inside now crystallized. I use a knife to coax a chunk out of its plastic prison and watch it crash into the pan like a meteor into the earth, which I've spent an unhealthy amount of time worrying might happen one of these days. Everything feels like it's on the precipice of disaster, or maybe it's just that I am, but it's all starting to feel the same. I can no longer differentiate the state of my mental health from the state of the world around me. Everything is ending and I'm terrified of what I'll lose when it does.

I already know I don't have the rose petals the recipe calls for. I don't have ashwagandha powder—I don't even know what it is. I do have cinnamon, though, so I add a pinch to the concoction before realizing I've accidentally scrolled down to a different recipe, but it's too late to go back now. I've spent all week trying a wide variety of so-called cure-alls anyway, tweaking each little by little when the first time didn't work. The melatonin tablets sat worthless in my stomach, the meditation videos made me sleepy but didn't make me sleep, the yoga left my muscles more exhausted than my brain. What's the worst this recipe could do? If anything, it'll just be another failed attempt I'll try to remedy tomorrow.

I whisk together the ingredients, pour the mixture into a mug. I swallow it down greedily, ignoring the burn in my throat, and wait for it to work its magic—or to realize I'm once again putting my faith into the wrong solution.

ELYSIAN

(adj.) blissful, delightful

———

MY FAVORITE MOMENTS are the ones that never seem noteworthy—the ones you never tell at parties or recount to your family, the ones that don't have a plot or reason. There's something in those excerpts of life, something so beautifully, achingly human. The sound of leaves crunching under your feet. The feel of a silk dress between your fingers. The brief glance you share with the stranger sitting across from you—a connection, if only for a moment. They are the building blocks of the human experience, the white noise that fills in all our blank spaces, and yet they're never what we tell our children. They're never what we think about when we reflect on our lives at the end of the day.

But my god, aren't they lovely? I want to collect them like scraps of paper and fold them into origami cranes. I want to stash them in my pockets to run my fingers over when I need to remind myself that sometimes, you don't need breathtaking, heart-racing moments to feel alive. Sometimes, the most mundane experiences are the most extraordinary.

ENNUI

(n.) a feeling of weariness or dissatisfaction

————

I DIDN'T FALL out of love with life all at once—instead, the disappointment fell like a single rain-drop against the windshield, barely noticeable, then continued again and again, one by one, faster and faster, and now I can't see anything else in front of me at all.

ENSORCELL

(v.) bewitch, enchant

———

IT IS A generational curse, to know what it takes to be loved.

I have inherited my mother's figure, how my flesh gives way at the slightest touch, shapeshifting into whatever I need to be. I have learned it's not about making yourself bigger or smaller, merely emptier—a vessel ready to hold whatever someone else no longer has it in them to carry. I carefully carve away those parts of me I've deemed dispensable—my boundaries, my exigencies, my particularities—until there's room to fit everything you ache to give me. In molding myself around you, I convince you not to leave.

It is harder than I thought it would be, becoming this pliant object, this collateral thing. It is a harrowing feeling, realizing I can make myself into something so unrecognizable that you never have to know me. And I am loved, I am loved, I am loved—but not the way I ever wanted to be.

EPHEMERAL

(adj.) lasting a very short time; a
transient or fleeting life cycle

———

WHEN YOU DIED, they gave me all your teacups.
It seemed like a quaint detail at first. While everyone
else sorted through your aging photographs, your
rosaries, your decades' worth of clothes, they would
find your finest china hiding in the back of a cabinet
or stashed in a box in the basement and set it aside
just for me. It was an honor to be left with some
of your most beautiful belongings—their ceramic
florals, their gold-tipped rims, their handles that spi-
raled out like a conch. Staring down at the treasure
laid at my feet, I couldn't imagine taking anything
more. I swaddled these remnants of you in terry
cloth and cradled them in my arms to carry home.

What a shame that now, years later, when I forget
the way you looked, the way you smelled, the way
your voice traced the sound of your favorite hymns,
I'll unwrap these final reminders of you, only to
find the porcelain chipped along the edges, cracked.
What a shame that I will love you for longer than I'll
know you and only be left with such delicate things.

EPOCH

(n.) an extended period of time usually characterized by a memorable series of events

———

I WOULD LIKE to move on if you'd ever let me, but you can't stop turning back the pages of our history. Every "I'm sorry" feels tedious now, a plea to absolve you of your guilt. To you, I have been etched in stone from years ago, a sign of your very worst times. Under your gaze, I feel myself memorializing, becoming the penance at the altar of your sins. But the person I was has been laid to rest; there's no mercy left to give. I am not a god; I am just a girl. Don't make me into something holier than I need to be.

ESTIVATE

(v.) to spend the summer usually at one place

————

THE SUMMER HEAT is suffocating, but it's not the only thing that's left me feeling stifled. Sometime between this year and last, I contracted a terminal restlessness, though I'm not sure where from. I'd rather be anywhere but here, but somehow here is the only place that exists for me until this season makes way for fall. I keep track of the passing seconds with the tapping of my foot, because even with nowhere to go, my body yearns for a freedom I never seem to find.

So when you call me in the middle of a Tuesday afternoon, asking if I want to go to the pool, I'm mostly just glad to have something to do that doesn't involve staring out the window, waiting for the nighttime to come. You pick me up in your Camry, but instead of driving to the community center, you head in the opposite direction.

"Where are we going?" I ask, perplexed.

You offer me a toothy smile, though I can't make out the rest of your expression from under the round sunglasses that eclipse most of your face. "You'll see."

I've never been patient enough to appreciate the element of surprise, but you love nothing more than to make a spectacle out of the everyday, and I know if I let you have this one, it'll be the most interesting thing to happen to me in weeks. I don't protest when we end up at the Korean market off 135th Street, where we fill a green plastic bag with kimbap and Hawaiian Sun—our favorite combination—and carry our treasures to the car. You head back toward my neighborhood, but when you drive past our usual pool, I can't help but shoot you a look. "Did I even need to wear a swimsuit?"

You shush me with a wave of your hand. "Come on, have I ever given you a reason not to trust me?"

No, I think, but that's never stopped me before. It's an old habit, this inclination to assume the worst, if only because I've found it easier to recover from the fall if I'm already anticipating it. In some ways, I've spent my whole life just waiting for the world to disappoint me. It isn't until now that I realize I don't want to be that way with you.

I try not to complain the rest of the way, a

Herculean effort on my part, though the tooth-marks on my tongue feel in vain when you park outside a wrought iron fence with a sign that reads, "Children's Aquatic Park."

"You're kidding me," I say, but you're already grabbing the plastic bag from my hand and climbing out of the car. "This place is for kids."

"So?" you shrug. "They're not going to kick us out."

"Not really my concern here," I mutter, which makes you laugh, but you don't wait around to see if I'll follow you in through the gate. You know better than most that I have nowhere better to be.

You pay for my admission and shepherd me through the entrance, leading me past the tangle of water-slides and straight toward the tide pool. "Sit," you order, pointing to an empty spot at the edge of the water, and I roll my eyes but obey, letting the manufactured waves lap up the length of my legs. Once you've settled beside me, your posture mir-roring mine, you set the kimbap on the beach towel between us, then pop the tabs of the Hawaiian Suns and hand one to me.

"All that fanfare just for this, huh?" I joke, taking the can.

You respond with a scalding look that rivals the heat rising from the concrete. "Just enjoy it," you say, but as soon as I take a sip of the drink, you add, "Now close your eyes."

I indulge you, letting the darkness of my eyelids and the taste of Guava on my tongue overtake me. With the sudden sensory loss comes an abrupt awareness of the soft clash of water against the cement, the birds cawing in the distance, the children laughing as their feet pad along the pool's edge. The sunrays singe my shoulders, my face, my legs, only to be quelled by the intermittent spray of the tides. I don't even notice the stillness that's settled into me until suddenly your voice is there, too, filled to the brim with a smile: "See, Toto? It's almost like we're not in Kansas anymore."

ESURIENT

(adj.) hungry, greedy

———

I'VE ALWAYS FOLLOWED the path carefully, fearing what it meant to stray. I tell myself there's safety in familiarity, that containment is the corridor to contentment, because curiosity may have killed the cat, but it cannot slaughter what it cannot catch. I tell myself there's safety in never needing more.

I've never known what to do with desire. I've always swallowed it down, trapped it inside, let it fester and ferment. But then there is you, whose eyes aim to excavate, whose words cut too deep, as if you know it'll take just one swing of the ax for it all to come spilling out. You've never feared the hunt, but even you can't predict the carnage that awaits you.

Because god, how I want and I want and I want. I lick the nectar from your wounds, but it's never enough to satiate my bloodlust, and even I begin to fear the monster you make of me. I was so afraid of becoming Little Red Riding Hood that I never noticed I'd become the wolf, mouth stained cherry red, teeth bared to bite into the whole of you.

ETHEREAL

(adj.) celestial, heavenly

———

THE TRAIN STATION is suffocating with people, and when the summer humidity slips in through the front door, it feels like we might drown in the commotion. Neither of us cares for crowds, so when you gesture me forward, I follow your cue and step outside, though I don't anticipate the disorientation that washes over me as soon as my shoes meet the sidewalk. The day has been perfectly clear, not a cloud in sight, but now the sky shimmers silvery above us; all we can do is blink up at it, confused, until I realize we have walked under some sort of awning that stretches out across the entirety of the lawn.

You point to a sign mounted on the fence. "It's an art installation."

On closer inspection, I notice the opaque netting above our heads, holding up hundreds—maybe thousands—of two-foot-long metallic streamers that dangle from the threads. They flutter in the springtime breeze, the sun shifting along every strand.

Like a bird, I'm compelled toward the shine, unable to stop myself from stepping forward. "Come on," I say, grabbing your arm and pulling you farther beneath it, continuing until silver surrounds us on all sides. There's something juvenile in my sense of wonder, in the spring of my step as I skip ahead of you. Before you have the chance to warn me the ground is wet, the way I already know you will, I drop down and lay belly-up in the grass.

"You're going to get dirty," you say, eyeing the way my nice dress splays around me, its long chiffon skirt pooling around my thighs.

"I'll wash up later," I retort.

You sigh but must find some merit in my logic because you plop down beside me, close enough that your elbow knocks against mine. "Sorry," you mutter, but I'm too delighted to be upset.

You take a breath. We have both grown quiet now, the noise from the station lost somewhere in the distance. Together, we stare up at the undulating ether, mesmerized by the way light filters in and reflects in all directions. It's like gazing into an ocean, the waves made of shimmering pearls. Or like a field full of wheat, grown silver instead of gold. Or like standing up close to a star, its blinding flames near enough I could touch them, if only I tried. As if to test the theory, I reach out into the air above me.

You glance over at me with a snort. "What are you doing?"

"Nothing," I lie, letting my arm fall back to my side.

You know me well enough that I know you don't believe me, but I appreciate that you don't press for another answer. Instead, you sigh. "I don't know the last time I felt this calm," you admit. "It kind of feels like being a kid again. I would've loved this back then."

Maybe it's the child that still lives inside me that reaches over to squeeze your arm. There's nothing more to say—the perfection of this moment transcends anything words could offer. Instead, we silently let the time pass us by, lost in the tranquility of this glimmering infinity. I already dread the moment you move, pulling me off the ground and plummeting me back to Earth.

EVANESCENT

(adj.) tending to vanish like vapor

———

SHE STRUMS HER GUITAR and the music filters down my spine, the notes like thin fingers stroking down the back of my neck. The chords hang in the air like chandeliers, glittering, lovely; they sink into my skin and vibrate through my bones.

I know this song—I know it—but I can't remember why it makes every joint inside me turn to stone. I forget how certain melodies can grab me by the collar and throw me against the wall.

Then I think: It was you. You used to play me this song, too.

There's something about winter nights in laundry rooms, the way you fumbled over the frets back when I swore I'd only ever sing for you. I think of the way your brow creased when you played, the way you concentrated on every curve of your fingers, the way you melted into the moment as if you belonged there, forever frozen in time.

The song haunted me even after the last strum of your guitar, even long after you left. It would follow me down sidewalks and echo in empty air as I sobbed on the bathroom floor when I realized you were gone, you were gone, you were really, truly gone.

But now I'm in this half-lit room that smells of incense and soy candles, and you aren't here, and you haven't been here in a while. Yet there it is: that song. Except now she's the one who plays it, and she summons it with deft fingers that make it feel foreign, new.

"Sing," she orders softly.

And so I do.

EXALT

(v.) to elevate by praise or in estimation

———————

THE MIRROR HOLDS you beautifully, which you would understand if you'd only just look. Instead, I sit on the other side of the room, trying to pretend I don't notice the way you turn from your reflection, refusing to meet your own gaze. "You look great," I assure you, but I can see the seeds of doubt stuck between the teeth of your answering smile.

How I wish I could make you understand. You might as well be a stranger to yourself because you've never studied the curve of your neck when you throw your head back and all your laughter spills out. You've never watched your eyebrows stitch together when you're lost deep in thought, the skin of your forehead wrinkling into ridges, adding texture to its softness. Even the way your fingers fidget when you're nervous entrances me, their rhythmic movements hypnotizing. Let me map out your freckles and I could prove there's a whole universe inside you. Let me bottle the lightning in your eyes and you will see how the whole room glows. Maybe then you'd believe me when I say that sometimes when I look at you, I ache.

Don't tell me there's nothing beautiful about you, not when you live and breathe in poetry. Don't tell me you're unlovable, not when I am living contradictory proof. You have made yourself so precious to me, so how can you say you have no value? It takes everything in me to stop myself from cradling your head in my hands, turning it back to the mirror and forcing you to face all the splendor I see.

FRORE

(adj.) frozen or frosty

———

I SAY I CAN'T STAND the winter, but what I mean is that I miss you and the way the steam curled off your lips when you'd taste the sound of my name. How your eyes would graze the sliver of thigh between my stockings and skirt and the skin would warm as if by your hands. I miss shivering from the anticipation, but instead of offering me a jacket, you'd use your arms as a shawl—your fingers smoldering like matchsticks, your breath engulfing me like smoke. I miss the winters when you were here because we never knew the cold— only shelter, only heat, only home.

GLOAMING

(n.) twilight

———

THE SUN IS SETTING on our time together, but I'm not ready to say goodnight. We find ourselves standing in a restaurant parking lot hours after we've finished our meal, kicking a discarded bottle cap back and forth with the toes of our shoes.

It always happens this way with us. No amount of time we're granted is ever enough. I want to tell you everything I possibly could, and if we run out of things to say, I want to tell you it all again, rehash every conversation, retrace every step. I never get tired of the things you have to say, even when I've heard it all before. I'm convinced we could be promised eternity and I would still be standing across from you on the blacktop, watching the sun sinking behind you and thinking, "I wish this would stop going by so fast."

But we don't have forever, only this waning evening and all the words I still haven't had the chance to share with you. Everyone around us is packing up their cars to leave, but still, we linger, always asking another question, always inserting one last aside. "I should probably go," you say, but you don't move, and neither do I. Our cars wait for us expectantly, but expectation always makes a rebel out of me, and I know deep down I would throw my keys into a river if there were only one nearby. Instead, I've run out of excuses, and we've run out of daylight, and there's nothing left to do but say goodbye.

HALCYON

*(adj.) characterized by happiness,
great success, and prosperity*

———

SOMETIMES WHEN I'M sitting out on the balcony, a book in one hand and a glass of wine in the other, I think: This is it. The breeze is knotting together the threads of my hair and the sunrays are burning my shoulders, and I know neither is supposed to be good for me, but it feels as delicious as a guilty pleasure. I love to close my eyes and take in these quiet moments that aren't really quiet at all because if I listen closely enough, the silence peels back just enough that I can hear a couple arguing from the apartment below mine; and if I listen even closer, I can hear the soft clink of ceramic meeting wood as they set the table for dinner because even in all their irritation, they will not make the other eat alone. And somewhere beyond that, children are laughing, throwing rocks into the river and sharing jokes I'd never understand because time seems to change everything except for the fact that kids always seem to speak their own secret language, and though I've lost my fluency, the sound of it still makes me smile. On days like these, the only things marking time are the church bells in the distance and the sun sinking below the horizon, staining the sky a vibrant orange that fades to inky blue. I try to track the way the colors change, the way the stars materialize as soon as there's nothing left to steal their light, until soon it's just me and the cosmos and the immensity of everything between us. What if I'd blinked and missed this? What if I'd gone inside? How much of the world has passed me by when I stopped paying attention? I'd never know to look for these moments if they weren't hidden in the places I was already planning to be, but the next time someone asks what it feels like to be happy, I'll think of this.

HELIOTROPISM

*(n.) phototropism in which sunlight
is the orienting stimulus*

————

AS THE SUMMER fades away and the sunflowers bloom, you ask me to go see them with you. We make the hour drive to the farm together, only for you to frown when we park along the dirt road. "They're facing away from us," you complain as we step out of the car.

You're right—we've made the mistake of coming at noon, when the sun is high in the center of the sky and every flower has turned its head toward it, seeking the rays of its validation. We wade out into the sea of thick stems anyway, tiptoeing around the bees that float above the leaves, reaching out to skim our fingertips along the silky petals that refuse to give us the time of day.

I can't fault the flowers too much. It's like when something funny happens and I reflexively look at you because nothing delights me more than when your face brightens and your gaze finds mine. Or how when you tell me a story and halfway through I'll realize my whole being has turned toward you, the line of our shoulders square, my disposition echoing yours, as if I've become a mirror. Or how sometimes I find myself rearranging my schedule so that I might run into you during your afternoon breaks, not because I need to or necessarily mean to, just because I have this unwitting urge to align my world with yours in the smallest ways. How can I blame nature for something it was created to do when even I can't stop myself from gravitating around you? From the day they bloomed, these flowers have followed their fate, and with you, I follow mine.

HYPERBOLE

(n.) extravagant exaggeration

————

"YOU'RE TOO MUCH," you tell me, the wrinkle in your brow reproving. I don't have to ask what you mean—you keep a verbal list of all the ways I exceed your expectations:

I am too loud.

I am too dramatic.

I am too needy.

I am too unrealistic.

I am too anxious.

I am too impulsive.

I am too obsessive.

I am too difficult to love.

I can't argue with your logic, not when, in many ways, you're right. I've never been a fan of limits, of stopping short of what I really mean. I don't want to know what it's like to live or love in half measures. I don't want to know what it's like to be anything less than everything.

HYPNAGOGIC

(adj.) of, relating to, or occurring in the period
of drowsiness immediately preceding sleep

———————

IN THE MIDDLE OF the night, when I grow
tired of chasing sleep, I find my breath meandering
after yours—slowly, softly. I'm always at a loss once
your eyes have closed because though you never
leave my side, I don't like that there are places you
go that I cannot follow. Even when there's no space
between us, there's always that chasm I cannot
cross, those parts of you I'll never reach, the pieces
that will always be unknowable to me. But maybe
if I lie here still enough, I can trace the pattern
of your heartbeat, let it lull me to a place no one
has ever gone before, where I'll find you between
reality and dream.

IMBROGLIO

(n.) an intricate or complicated situation

––––––––

SOMETIMES I WONDER if we live in parallel worlds, if those thousands of miles between us only act as a mirror. When I get up to make my coffee in the morning, I know you're also pouring honey into the bottom of your mug, just enough to make the bitter grounds taste sweet, the way you once showed me how to do. When I pull a brush through my hair, you're threading your fingers through yours, neither of us ever satisfied with the results; and when we check our phones for messages, we always frown at the exact same time, disappointed by the silence that's no longer become a surprise. When I lie in bed at night, searching for sleep, are you halfway across the country, reaching into the empty spaces of your mattress, too? As I pass the hours of the night dreaming of you, are you curled up on your side just as I am, dreaming of her?

INEFFABLE

(adj.) incapable of being expressed in words

————

THE WINDOWS IN the buildings surrounding us darken as the city settles into sleep, and though we're far from joining them, the silence has already found its way between us. Every halfhearted joke we try to throw back and forth falls flat to the floor, and neither of us has the heart to keep ignoring them, so instead, we preoccupy ourselves with disassembling the pieces of this stage of your life. I pretend I don't notice you trying not to cry, though when your eyes meet mine, I'm surprised by my urge to blink back tears, too—I am not used to saying goodbyes, and I don't know how to make myself ready for you.

In the darkest hours of the night, as we pack the last of your memories away into your trunk, you turn to me, suddenly resolute. "One last fun thing before we leave?" I answer by climbing into the passenger seat.

You don't tell me where we're going, and I can't bring myself to ask—the silence between us feels too fragile, and I don't want to be the one who breaks it.

I swallow back my confusion as you drive us to the top of the empty parking garage, don't even question it when you exit the car and beckon me to follow. It isn't until you rummage through the backseat and pull out four rolls of streamers that I can't hold back my voice anymore. "What is *that* for?"

For the first time all night, the edges of your lips curl into a smile. "You'll have to see."

You lead me to the tall concrete structure at the edge of the lot, though you hesitate when you glance back at me. "Maybe this isn't a great idea," you say. "You're wearing a skirt."

But my curiosity has been piqued, and though I'd never admit it aloud, I'm not ready to leave yet. Once we're gone, I don't know when I'll see you again; when I do, I don't know what will change. That uncertainty pools into the floor of my stomach, solidifying like cement, but I refuse to let you see. Instead, I brave a wry look and say, "Like I would ever let that stop me."

You help hoist me onto the roof, and when I straighten up and stare over the town we've come to call home, I understand why you brought me here. The night has been heavy with darkness, but in the distance, there is only light—from the city, from the passing headlights, from the stars. There is a magic in seeing our everyday world from above.

You climb up beside me, handing me half the streamers. Standing side-by-side, I inherently seem to know what you want from me.

"Ready?" you ask.

"Ready," I confirm.

As we launch them into the air, for a moment, the night is breathtaking; but then the fluttering reds and blues tangle into the trees, and my gut is still tangled up in dread. Whatever cinematic moment we'd been hoping for passed in a flash; whatever release we needed didn't come. Now it's just you and me on a parking garage roof, overlooking everything we're leaving behind, with nowhere left to go but away from each other.

"I'm afraid of losing touch with people," I blurt out, though what I really mean is I'm afraid of losing you. It's not until I've put the words out there that I realize how badly I've been wanting to say them, though the truth of them terrifies me almost as much as it does to give you this window of insight into my brain, into what this means to me.

You pause, soaking in what I've just said, because I've broken through something we've spent all day preserving and neither of us can ignore it anymore.

"I hate when people say we lose things from our lives because they didn't matter," you say slowly, as if testing the weight of every word. "They did matter. We do."

As we stare down at those streamers in the trees, our mark on this world that will be gone by the time it rains tomorrow, our silence speaks louder than either of us ever could. I don't tell you I already know I'll drive back by this spot in the morning, that I'll leave my car at the curb and climb up the base of the tree just to pluck a piece of those paper ribbons from its branches. I can't explain how I already feel the night slipping through my fingers, how I know the years are soon to follow, but I'll fold this scrap of streamer into my journal to preserve for as long as I live. Every inch of this city might forget about us, and maybe you will, too, but I will your words to become true. Even if nothing else does, these hands will always hold the proof that we mattered.

INFATUATED

(adj.) filled with extravagant love or admiration

———

I AM IN MY element: a cup of some unspecified liquor in my hand, dark lipstick smeared across my smile. My hair is a wild nest that swirls around my shoulders while I sway through the room—"It's how we gauge how many drinks you've had," you told me once, "the crazier the hair, the drunker." I pinball from person to person, laughing at the banter exchanged, though I somehow always end up right back beside you.

You watch me, amused, as I tell you about the man I met when refilling my drink in the kitchen, how I'd asked him what he'd choose to do with his life if he was allowed to do anything and he'd replied, "I'd be a carpenter."

"Why doesn't he do it?" I ask you, taking another swig from my cup. "No one's stopping him. He said it would make him happier than anything! And it's attainable! Maybe I should go find him and tell him that."

You laugh a little, then shake your head. "I just realized something about you."

I look over at you, more startled than confused by this sudden digression. "What?"

You shake your head like you've surprised yourself by saying it, too. "I think you fall in love with every person you meet for a minute or two." With a self-conscious shrug, you add, "I don't mean, like, romantically. Just in a way."

Your words spin through my inebriated brain, and even as I struggle to grasp on to them, I feel something click into place. Is that what this is? That spark of connection you feel when you cross paths with someone new. That anticipation that comes with not yet knowing how a stranger will fit into the jigsaw of your life but realizing they could change its shape permanently. That insatiable curiosity that comes with knowing there is a well of information before you, if only you're brave enough to dip the bucket deeper. That yearning to see someone for exactly what they are—and to see yourself reflected back in them, too.

I think of that man who could be a carpenter but considers it a hypothetical, how I'll probably never see him again but how I so badly need to know he's happy. How maybe we all have this urge to see the people around us living well, even in the smallest ways, and that's why we hold doors open for those walking behind us and why we compliment passersby on the street and why we ask strangers questions about themselves, even though we know the answers will never really affect us. Maybe we spend our whole lives falling in love with each other—just in a way, just for a minute or two.

INGÉNUE

(n.) a naïve young woman

————

"TRUST ME," you whisper to me with that Cheshire cat grin.

So I hold your hand as you pull me down the rabbit hole again.

INSOUCIANCE

(n.) nonchalance

———————

WE ARE SITTING across from each other at the table—me writing, you working—when I feel your attention reach out to graze the edges of my face. Sure enough, when I look up, you're looking back at me, and we both freeze in the headlights of the other's gaze, mortified by our carelessness.

I am the first to find my composure, so I clear my throat and shift uncomfortably under your scrutiny. "Don't look at me like that."

But I've made the fatal error of acknowledging this thing that's been growing between us, the one we've made an unspoken vow to avoid at all costs. By the time I've realized it, it's too late—the words begin to feed off the oxygen between us.

You curl your fist against the oak tabletop, attempt to take in a breath. "Like what?"

Like I hold the sun in the cradle of my ribcage and

you're a moth to the light. Like it's my hands that lie on the face of the clock, the only thing moving time forward. Like you've already started building my pedestal, one of the perfect height to idolize me from first and to push me from later, if only I give you the chance.

"Like nothing," I say and look away.

INURE

(v.) to accustom to accept something undesirable

———

I DON'T WANT TO be this angry person, but every day something comes along to stoke the coals in my chest. There is no amount of screaming that ever lets off enough steam, so instead, I'm forced to let the pressure build as I try to choke it down, swallow it whole. But these veins carry something volatile, twisting together like the wires of a time bomb that's become too easily triggered. I am combustible, destructible, one lit match away from obliterating anything within a twenty-mile radius, erasing every trace of me with it. I look in the mirror to try to find the softness I used to hold, but all I see is white-hot rage, and some days I'm convinced that's all I'm ever going to be.

IRENIC

(adj.) favoring, conducive to, or operating
toward peace, moderation, or conciliation

————

THE WALLS OF this house are one argument away from crumbling, but these war-torn years have made a martyr out of me. I will scream at the top of my lungs and break all the dishes if that's the bomb that will put a stop to all this fighting; I will apologize a thousand times and sweep the wreckage from the floor if you promise to forgive me. And if that's not enough, I will make myself whatever size you prefer me to be—bigger if you need an easier target to aim for, smaller if you need more space to breathe. Tell me how to fix these damaged founda- tions and I will work my hands raw, my muscles bruised and aching, till every bone in this tired body is on the verge of breaking. I can choose to be crushed under the rubble when the roof comes caving in, or I can collapse under the weight of holding this home together—at least then there will be something still left standing once the dust settles, even though I've given up hope that it could ever be me.

LABYRINTHINE

(adj.) of, relating to, or resembling a
labyrinth; winding, maze-like

———

I'VE STARTED LOSING track of night and day
because, through the lens of my depression, it all starts
to look the same. Whether or not the sun is out, I'm
counting the tiles in the ceiling—thirty-six, there are
always thirty-six—and wondering when they'll finally
come crashing down on me. I used to spend my mid-
nights searching for silver linings, those promises of
light behind every shadow, only to realize that in my
hunt for an exit, I have dug myself too deep. I try to
retrace my footsteps, try to figure out where I took
the wrong turn, hoping that maybe this time I'll notice
something new—a sign, a promise, a crack in these god-
forsaken ceiling tiles—but knowing I won't, because
I've spent too many hours bargaining with every being
that might be listening to believe anything can hear
me from here. So I'll just keep pacing back and forth
between dead-end and dead-end, carving trenches into
the floorboards with these blistered feet, because the
only thing worse than this fruitless pursuit is the real-
ization that my only other option is to stop.

LACHRYMOSE

(adj.) given to tears or weeping

———

THERE IS NOTHING worse than watching the ones you love ache. I will hold your hand as the sobs rock your body, an earthquake that cracks the dam as all your grief spills out. I do not know how to collect the shards of you that lay waiting for someone to hold them, I do not know how to stop the waves of snot and spit and tears, so I will sit by your side, staring at blank spaces on the wall, because there is something too intimate about looking at a man who has carved himself empty and left his bloodied remains on the linoleum floor.

LACUNA

(n.) a blank space or a missing part

———

"DO YOU FEEL like doing something stupid?" you ask me out of nowhere.

I look over to where you're sitting beside me at our workstation, eyebrow raised. I make a mental catalog of the last twenty-four hours: How, when we found ourselves without a place to stay for the night, we pretended to lock up the storefront of the shop, then walked to the nearest bar for as many Aperol Spritzes as we could drink within the hour. How you chain-smoked a pack of cigarettes we bought off a group of teenagers and flipped off any man who leered at us as we staggered to the bodega, where we flirted shamelessly with the cashier till he sold us two bottles of wine and a jar of Nutella. How we snuck back into the shop, avoiding all the security cameras we'd spent the last few months clocking, and made a bed out of the backroom floor. How we sat across from one another, passing the wine and Nutella back and forth, and by the time sunlight leaked through the display window, we hadn't yet slept, but I knew about your father's infidelity and you'd learned the full story about the scar beneath my eyebrow. How we took showers in the bathroom sink and downed three espressos each, then snuck back out of the shop so we could show up an hour later, pretending to arrive for our shifts.

Do I feel like doing something stupid? "Obviously."

On our lunch break, we walk to the tattoo parlor, planning out exactly how we want to commemorate our impromptu night together.

"I've got this quote from an Italian poem I love," I tell you. "I want it on my back shoulder."

"Nice," you approve. "I'm going to get a hand holding up its middle finger."

"Where?" I ask.

"On my ass."

I'm not sure if it's the delirium that keeps us laughing for as long as we do, but we don't stop till we get to the tattoo parlor and you come to a sudden halt, frowning.

"What?" I ask, trying to see what's disappointed you, but it takes me a moment to notice the little paper sign on the door: "Closed for the rest of the month."

"Bummer," you say, then shrug, turning on your heel. "Oh well, we tried."

"I'm sure we'll find something else stupid to do," I agree.

You grin back. "I'd be disappointed in us if we didn't."

As we walk back to the shop, I rub the back of my shoulder, the skin tingling as if it's already been marked. Even without the ink, even if no one else will ever be able to see it, I'll know I'll always feel the message there: *Quant'è bella giovinezza*—how beautiful is youth.

LANGUISH

(v.) to be or live in a state of depression or decline

———

"WHEN YOU MISS one train," you tell me, "you just have to catch the next."

But I've been standing in place for so long I'm convinced every track has been left abandoned. I watch the world pass me by, my feet drying into the concrete floors, my baggage growing too heavy to hold. I would buy every first-class ticket they'd sell me if only there were any use. Instead, I watch the clock on the wall move faster than I ever will, resigned to the fact that I'll never escape this station.

LILT

(v.) to move in a lively manner

————

WE ORDER TWO glasses of prosecco in Santo Spirito and settle in along the curb. Yesterday we were strangers, but these Florentine streets have worked their magic, and suddenly we speak in the coded language of old friends. Under the glow of the streetlamps, I swear I must have known you long before we ever met.

You're telling me a story about your mother when the music floats toward us from over by the Basilica, and the moment you register the sound, your whole face transforms. You leave your sentence behind, forgotten. "It's salsa music," you inform me, your eyes glittering. When you notice my perplexed look, you add, "I'm a dancer."

Now that I know this small fact, there is suddenly a whole new layer to you: You learned about salsa in South America, where you studied abroad for a year. You don't speak Italian, but you're fluent in Portuguese, which is why you seem to understand fragments of everything we hear around us, my translations only confirming what you already know. You love languages so much you dedicated your life to studying them, but it's really the dancing that stuck with you; when you returned to the States, you started taking classes every week.

"You should join them," I tell you, nodding my head toward the crowd of people that has already started forming in the square.

Your smile falls just a little, just enough, but you hide it with a shrug. "I don't know. I haven't danced in a while." You are offering me another layer to peel, though at first, it's difficult to grasp. That is, until you admit, "My boyfriend doesn't like it."

But don't you? I want to ask, as if I don't already know the answer, as if it won't be painful enough for either of us to hear. Instead, I gulp down my prosecco and, gathering up the rest of my courage, ask, "Will you teach me?" The smile you reward me with is enough to ease my apprehension.

We abandon our empty glasses on the sidewalk and stumble into the square, giddy from the alcohol bubbling in our veins. You put both of your hands on my shoulders to guide me to where I'm supposed to stand, directing my movements step-by-step. I can't stop laughing as I stumble over my own feet, but you exist within the music as if you're part of it, seamlessly weaving your way around the piazza, twisting around me with a grin.

It hits me that maybe I didn't really know you until this moment, because I am so bad at this, but you are so good, so at home with the world around you, so at home with who you are in a way I've never seen before. I have the sudden urge to be the one who puts my hands on your shoulders, who orders you to stop, only for a moment, just long enough to make you listen when I say, "Please, do not give up this piece of you for anything."

LYCANTHROPE

(n.) a werewolf

———

WE BUILD A BONFIRE in the backyard from scraps of whatever we can find, feed the flames till they flicker and dance in the glow. We are too young to be playing with fire and too old not to know we shouldn't, but there's something inside me that thirsts to watch the world burn.

I'm not sure when I lost all my softness, when I began to crave the idea of pulling away the last of my vulnerable flesh to let myself become all bones, all brutality. I'm not sure when the hunger began, but there is a ravenousness in me I cannot quell—too much need, too much want, but not enough of anything to satisfy me.

So I sharpen my fangs, howl at the moon, puff out my chest to make myself as big as I can because I don't want to admit how small I've become, how fragile, and because people cannot break what they're too afraid to touch. I start to convince myself that this is what it means to be strong, even though the truth is that I'm uncertain, that I'm scared, that even I don't recognize what I transform into when bathed in the spotlight of the night. Am I this blood-thirsty creature or the small, timid girl I become in the daylight? Could there have ever been a Jekyll if there hadn't been a Hyde? After all, it's only in these witching hours that I am totally feral, free.

MACKLE

(v.) blur

———

YOUR VOICE USED to murmur like a violin, or at least I think it did. I haven't heard it in years, and I haven't heard from you in even longer. Sometimes I think about the day we stole all the kiwis from the kitchen and had a feast out on the lawn, except maybe it was oranges, except maybe it wasn't you. When I remember you now, it's like a patchwork quilt, all these scraps of moments held together in a mismatched pattern. Or maybe it's like when you pose for a picture, and then someone makes a joke, and then everyone is laughing so hard the photograph comes out blurry, all our edges gone soft. When I find it years later pressed between the pages of a book, I can't make out our faces, I can't hear our laughter, I can't remember what we found so funny in the first place—all the details fall away from me, fuzzy. But I remember how it all felt. Oh, how could I ever forget how this feels?

MELLIFLUOUS

(adj.) having a smooth rich flow

———

TIME RUSHES PAST us on the interstate, but it seems irrelevant when I'm sitting next to you. I'm not sure if it's been two hours or ten, just that it's been long enough for us to have taken the space between the windshield and the back bumper and built our own little universe. I'm not sure it will survive in the suffocating air outside of this moment, but for now, it's just us, just the music from the radio and the stars stretched above our heads and the liminal space that is the countryside in the middle of winter. I tell myself it is enough for me.

A song crackles through the static, so quiet I don't hear it at first; when I finally recognize the beat, my heart swells. It's the one that played the night we met, the one that once made you look at me like a madwoman when you realized I knew every word. I reach out to turn up the volume, but in the dark, I find your fingers already on the dial. I hate that we pull away in tandem, as if recoiling from an electric shock. I hate that time doesn't stop, even when my heartbeat does.

"This is my favorite," I say, gesturing toward the radio, as if this might explain why my foot has stuttered on the gas pedal, why I feel the sudden urge to hit the brakes and live on this midnight road forever.

I hear the cosmos expanding in your voice when you say, "I remember."

You reach out again—carefully, as if one wrong move might destabilize our atmosphere—and turn up the music. I mouth along to the lyrics, silently at first, but when I feel you watching me, it's like you've twisted the dial in my throat, too. You laugh as I match every word that floats from the speakers, your joy harmonizing with mine.

When the song ends, you grab your phone from the console between us. "Can I play one for you, too?"

I've never heard the song that starts to hum through the air; this time, we both grow quiet as the melody thrums between us. I hold my breath for fear of somehow disturbing this moment, of missing a single beat, because I know there is a message hidden somewhere underneath. I listen as the lyrics tell the story neither of us has it in our heart to write—a love letter to this night, to me, to you.

MOIETY

(n.) one of two equal parts

———

THE FIRST DAY I move into my apartment in Italy—coincidentally, the same exact one you lived in two summers ago—I call to tell you. "Oh, via della Pergola," you sigh wistfully through the receiver. "I could tattoo that address straight onto my skin."

When we hang up, I send you videos of my room—where you used to fall asleep every night—and of the cat—the one who would eat lettuce straight from your plate—and you tell me exactly where to walk to buy the best gelato. I am a thousand miles away from any semblance of home, but as I bite into your favorite flavor, I understand how you must've felt when you stood in this spot.

Every day I send you a picture of someplace I find beautiful, and every time you reply, "Oh, I loved it there!" For every new experience I tell you about, you have a story to match. You ask me to find your favorite olive oil shop, the one you stumbled upon by accident on some obscure dead-end street; I'm delighted when I realize it's only a few shops down from the boutique where I work. I tell you about an artist I met while she was peddling paintings by the river; you say, "I bought something from her, too!" I start to realize every doorstep I pass is one you've walked by before. Every corner of this city I find has been discovered by you first.

Soon it starts to feel like time is thinning between us, because every conversation we have brings us closer until there's almost no distance between now and then. Sometimes when I'm walking these streets, I can't shake the feeling that you're here, too, your past and my present existing in tandem, as if I might turn the corner at any moment and run face-first into you. Together, we exist nonlinearly.

But we're thrown back into reality all at once: the day I return home is your last day in town before you move away. When we meet up one final time, each of us has one foot planted somewhere else. Maybe it's this sense of unsteadiness that makes me ask, "Did you mean what you said before?"

We show up at the tattoo parlor unannounced, and though they say they see customers on an ap-pointment-only basis, they tell us someone has just conveniently canceled theirs. We exchange glances, nervous but knowing fate has already intervened enough between us that we would be fools not to recognize this sign, too.

After months of letting you pave the way for me, I volunteer to sit in the leather chair first. When our artist asks where I want the tattoo, I point to the expanse of skin we have agreed on: each our right foot, the part of us that touched foreign soil first.

As the needle scratches my skin, it's easy to forget that we'll never know the same home again. Soon, we will move to opposite ends of the country—you to the west, me to the east—and our lives will become untwined as quickly as they wound together. I will begin walking past buildings you've never seen before; you will meet people I'll never have the chance to know. But I also know there will be days when we stand up at the exact same time, and when our feet touch the ground, our tattoos will align, and for the briefest second, the years and the miles that have woven themselves between us won't even matter. In certain inexplicable ways, we will always be bound together.

MOXIE

(n.) courage, determination

———

WE TELL OUR PARENTS we're going swim-
ming at the cracked concrete motel pool, but the
moment we leave the house, your smirk betrays you.
You hold up the keys to your parents' old Corolla,
shaking them so the metal sings like wind chimes.
"Want to go on a little adventure?"

I hesitate at the passenger door of the car, but when
you climb in, I know I have no choice. You may be
the troublemaker, but I'm the one you've always
chosen to shine your light on—your brightness is
both blinding and illuminating, and against my bet-
ter judgment, I have vowed to follow it anywhere.

This time it takes us to the woods along the edges of
the empty small-town parking lot, the kind of place
I'd otherwise avoid at all costs. As if sensing my res-
ervations, you turn to me and ask, "Are you scared?"

Always, I want to say. The older I get, the darker
the world seems to become, and while I no longer

believe in the monsters under my bed, I seem to find them everywhere else. But you have never been afraid of anything, or at the very least, you've always refused to show it, your bravery acting as an armor I've always envied. I shake my head and brace myself as we disappear into the trees.

You lead us through patches of thorns that tear at our ankles, over fallen trees that threaten to cave under our weight. You never flinch, never hesitate, only continue down some invisible path without waiting to see if I'm still behind you because there has never been a time when I haven't aligned my footprints perfectly with yours.

"You're going to love this," you tell me, then add, "just be careful of the leeches."

After five or so minutes of walking, I finally hear it: the rushing sound of water somewhere up ahead. As the trees begin to thin, a river takes its place, its murky water bubbling up from a crevice in the ground. There are already two people wading in it, boys who look much older than me but who know you by name.

As we strip down to our swimsuits—me more self-consciously than you—you introduce us. "She's a city girl," you tell them, jerking your head toward me.

"I could've told you that," one of them says, and everyone laughs but me.

You show me the rope tied to one of the tree branches overhanging the river, explain that it's the best way to jump in. "You don't have to if you're scared, though," you amend.

I don't really care to, but I seem to understand that saying no means something more to everyone here, and I don't want to disappoint you by disappointing them. So I grab the rope and jump, though I lose my grip halfway through and go crashing into the water, spluttering. I come up for air to the sound of laughter. "It's not for everyone," one of the boys assures me, which somehow makes me feel worse.

"I want to try again," I say to everyone's surprise.

I climb out of the water and up the muddy bank, pulling at the exposed tree roots to help me find my footing. I take the rope from you again, but this time my hands are so slick with muck that I fall into the river almost immediately.

"It's fine," you assure me when I resurface, but it's not—not to me. A certain determination has settled into me that I'm not used to feeling, and I'm unsure if it's because I need your approval or because I have an audience or just because I'm tired of being so cautious for someone who's still so young. I'm tired of being nothing but a shadow in your spotlight, the angel on your shoulder to your devil on mine. I'm tired of being timid, unassuming me.

I clamber back up again, taking extra caution to wipe my hands against my thighs before tightening my grip on the rope. When I pull backward and jump up so that my feet are secure around the knot at the base of the cord, I hold on with everything in me.

As the world rushes past me, I don't even realize that I'm laughing until I hear your voice over the sound of it: "Let go!" you yell, and so I do, letting myself fly through the air and cannonball into the water. This time, I come up gasping, and all I hear are the cheers around me.

"Pretty brave for a city girl," one of the boys tells me.

When I look up at where you're standing on the bank, I can see the pride in your smile as you say, "I could've told you that."

NEBULOUS

(adj.) indistinct, vague

———

THE THICKET OF CLOUDS follows our ascent up the mountain, creeping behind us like an ever-present shadow. You're determined to make it to the peak, even when it starts to rain, because you've dreamed of what you've been told you can see from the top.

"It'll be worth it," you assure me. "Every picture I've seen is gorgeous."

I'm not entirely convinced, but you've been talking about this day for weeks, so I don't bother voicing my reservations. As the thunder begins to rumble around us, you paint me a picture of surrounding mountains that rise up to meet us and a river that snakes below like a ribbon. You promise the discomfort of the present is just a small price to pay for the future reward—how someday, we won't even remember the storm.

But the clouds are faster than the both of us; when we reach our destination, they've already settled in, coloring the view an impenetrable gray. It isn't until we toe the edge of the cliff that the clouded wall begins to take on its own life, transforming into a shifting, murky abyss—as if all it would take is just one more step forward to become completely lost from the Earth. The longer I stare into it, the more I seem to lose my sense of self, as if I've begun to dissipate into the gloom.

"What a waste," you say, turning away.

This time, I cannot bring myself to follow you, not when it means ripping my eyes away from the thick wall of obscurity surrounding us. For once, it feels like I'm seeing the world as it really is—unfathomable and endless. There are no mountains or rivers or endless skies in sight, but we are standing on the edge of something immense—something I know I'll never forget. I want to pull you back and ask if you feel this way, too, but you are already retracing our steps to where we came from, your back turned to the view. You cannot see past your expectations, just as I cannot see past this void, and though we did not get what we came looking for, I know I will spend the next few weeks dreaming in grayscale.

NEPENTHE

(n.) something capable of causing
oblivion of grief or suffering

———

YOU PICK ME UP outside of my house, but when I ask you where we're going, you shrug. "Who knows?" you reply. "Anywhere."

It's only when I climb in beside you that I realize your grief is on the driver's side, its hands strangling the wheel. You let it take us to the highway, where we drive straight ahead till the sky wrings out the sunlight and we start to lose our sense of direction. But I don't have the vocabulary to ask if you're okay, not when I already know the answer, and pretending otherwise would feel like an insult to us both. Instead, the only words on my lips are the lyrics to the fuzzy song blaring through the radio; when I finally hear you sing along, it doesn't seem to matter that we have no idea where we're going, just that we're together, just that you're not shut inside that empty house alone. So when you see the ramp to Nebraska and turn onto it impulsively, all I can do is shrug and say, "I've heard that's a nice place," and I don't know if that's true, but for you, I need it to be.

When we finally see the lights of some town we've never seen before twinkling in the distance, we move toward them like they're the beacon that will save us from this incurable darkness. "It's like the glimmering hope of New York City," I tell you, then amend, "but significantly more underwhelming," and we're so exhausted that we laugh until the car finally rolls into this foreign land we swear we must be the first to ever find. We buy milkshakes at the only open diner before we say goodbye to this midnight Midwestern refuge, this corner of the country that will cease to exist the moment it disappears from the rearview mirror, and I silently thank it for letting you bring me here so it could finally bring you back to me.

NIVEOUS

(adj.) snowy

————

I STARE OUT AT the blizzard raging outside this little house in the middle of nowhere, the one we drove six hours to hide out in for the week. "How much do you think we'll get?" I ask.

"They say it could be a few feet," you tell me without looking up from your phone.

I don't know who "they" are, but I begin secretly hoping they're right, even as I voice my concerns about losing power. "Only we would get stranded in the middle of nowhere the day before Thanksgiving," I say, hoping my exhilaration sounds more like misery.

Later, you try to open the front door but realize the storm has rendered the solid wood unmovable. "Hopefully, we'll have better luck tomorrow," you say, but I am already busy making hot chocolate in the kitchen, humming along to a song I've queued up on the stereo.

"We can wait it out," I tell you, as if patience is suddenly my virtue.

Before I burrow into bed that night, I find myself staring out the window again, entranced by the ice accumulating on the sill. I fantasize about waking up in the morning and finding the whole house has been buried beneath it, every exit transformed into a wall of shimmering white. Hundreds of miles from here, our families anticipate our arrival, but I would rather be stuck frozen in time, two smiling figures held captive in a snow globe, kept safe from the ways the world will change us when we're forced back out into reality.

NOCTUARY

(n.) a journal of nocturnal incidents

———

IN THESE RESTLESS years, the ones where I no longer sleep and you feel stifled by your stagnancy, we start a new nighttime routine: We buy the 7 o'clock bus tickets to Chicago and meet when the sun begins to set at the station, which is really just an empty parking lot across from the Chinese supermarket. We each bring one suitcase of all our favorite outfits—"They're wasted on this town, anyway," you always say—and a backpack of things we want to share with each other: lychee jellies, a notebook of handwritten poetry, last month's *Vogue*, a bag of chips with a language I can't identify printed on the package. When the bus pulls away from the curb, we're always ecstatic, if only at the thought of leaving everything we've ever known behind, even if we're doomed to return. In those first few hours, we always speak in secrets that darken with the sky— those things we only feel safe saying in the limbo of moquette seats and rattling windows, displaced from time and space, from my heartbreak and that job you hate. It's easier to admit the truth when the only people listening are strangers only by technical-ity because everyone here seems to be running from something, and in that way, we're all the same. At some point, we stop in St. Louis, and we grow quiet then, listening to the movement around us, to the passengers who stalk up and down the aisles, unable to sit still anymore, and the quiet groans of tired patrons growing impatient to get back on the road. When we finally move again, the droning bus engine lulls you to sleep, and I stare out at the blur of the night and try to count the stars. Even when everyone else grows still around me, my insomniac mind can never quiet long enough to drift off—not now, not when there's a whole world on the other side of this pane of glass. You always wake up right outside the city limit, like clockwork, and like clockwork, when you ask me how I slept, I always shrug. We never say anything more till the bus doors finally open again and we step out into this new land, purified by the flames of the sunrise—reborn.

OBLIVION

(n.) a state marked by lack of
awareness or consciousness

————

I KEEP TRYING to reach you, but you've changed the locks again, hid the spare key. I know you're in there somewhere, lost within the darkness, but you don't answer when I knock.

I've grown used to you shutting me out, but this is something different—this vicious silence, this agonizing resistance. I try to kick down the door, but it doesn't budge, no matter how many names I call it. I claw at windows, try to force the shutters open, but they've been painted shut. Even the fence has become impossible to scale, a battlement designed to deter us both. The harder I try to break in, the more I start to worry you'll never see the outside of these walls again.

Don't you hear me out here? I am ringing the doorbell, yelling your name. Don't you see me out here? I am pointing my flashlight through the cracks in the blinds, urging you to follow the glow. Don't you know I'm out here? I'm begging you to let me in, but every plea just comes echoing back. You don't notice me standing on the other side, promising I won't leave you, I'm never going to leave you, even if you never open the door for me again.

OFFING

(n.) the part of the deep sea seen from the shore

———

WHEN THE WAVES come crashing toward the shore, I rush forward to meet them, unaware that you've already retreated to the safety of dry land. I can't say I'm surprised—it's a tale as old as time: While I long to dissipate into the sea foam, to lose myself in my element, you have always been a creature of the earth. We've always been different in these fundamental ways, but it's easy to forget that when I'm standing next to you.

"I can't believe you're afraid of the ocean," I say, falling back just enough to elbow you lightly, and I notice the way you jump at the touch.

"It's freaky," you reply defensively, rubbing the watery imprint off your arm. "You never know what's under the surface."

So what? I want to say. Is there anything that's ever truly what it seems? I still remember the first day I met you, how your strong exterior never betrayed your warmth, but even at your coldest, I never feared what might lie underneath. Now that I have seen the softness of your underbelly, I realize I never could have known you any other way. Is that so different? I want to ask. But you would never understand. After all, I was always the open book, always willing to brave the fishbowl of your scrutiny if it meant earning your trust.

I step out into the water, glancing over my shoulder just long enough to grin at you. "Well, I'm not scared of anything."

We both know it's a lie—you know spiders make me squirm; you know I cover my eyes the moment I see blood, even if it's on TV; you know I don't like being left alone in any place I've convinced myself is haunted. But even you don't understand the depths of my anxiety, the way it extends to the edges of nearly everything. Because I'm terrified of all the goodbyes I'll never get to say. I'm terrified of working toward the things I want, only to realize they never made me happy in the first place. And I may not be scared of you—never of you—but I'm terrified of how I can't seem to figure out what we are to each other. I'm terrified of the fact that I traveled all this way with you, and I'm terrified of going home because I'm not sure what will change in the hundreds of miles between here and there, but I'm worried it'll be everything—or worse, nothing at all. I'm terrified of the thought that maybe we were only ever meant to exist in the in-betweens.

But you don't know that, so all you can do is watch as I wade out into the water, letting the waves pull me farther and farther away from you. It's impossible for me to be afraid of the ocean, not when I can lie back and close my eyes and forget there's anything here to be afraid of at all. There's something comforting in knowing there's one thing there's no point in even trying to control.

"Wait," I hear you say, your voice far away.

I open my eyes again, squinting out past the sun, and see you're already waist-deep in the water. I'm so surprised that I try to stand upright suddenly, my feet kicking as they search for the ocean floor; you reach out to help me find my footing. We're so caught up in the moment that we don't notice when the water surges around us, knocking us both off balance and pulling us under the surface.

When I reemerge, I rub the salt from my eyes and reach for you, find you spluttering for air. "Are you okay?" I ask, spitting out the grit from between my teeth, and you respond with a gasping breath that leaves your lungs as laughter. Then suddenly, I'm laughing with you, the two of us howling louder than the crashing of the tides.

When we finally pull ourselves together, I look to see you grinning at me as if all your anxiety has washed away, disappearing with my own. We don't think twice before we throw ourselves into the waves again, letting them carry us wherever they may.

ORPHIC

(adj.) mystic, oracular

———

THE NIGHT BEFORE they find you on the floor beside the fireplace, unmoving, you visit me in a dream. You cup my face in the still-warm palms of your hands, have not yet lost the strength you need to pull me into your lap. There is a familiar sense of safety in your embrace until you tell me, "I won't be here for very long."

I want to ask you why, but the words don't seem to exist in this dreamscape—or maybe it's that I won't let them, because I refuse to understand the vocabulary of abandonment, not in the scope of my own unconsciousness. I refuse to know the questions whose answers will only break my heart.

"I want you to know you'll be okay without me," you say, stroking your fingers through my hair, as if to quell the waves of discomfort that have started churning inside of my gut. "Even if it doesn't feel like you will be, you'll be okay."

But how can you know that? I have never lived in a world without you, but neither have you. I'm not convinced there's ever been a time that has existed where you are not somewhere in it, rolling your cigarettes on the kitchen table, laughing at some joke you've made in your head. I silently vow I'll do everything in my power to make sure there never is because, in all of human history, there has never been a smile quite like yours.

When I wake up in the early morning haze, your words have already started to slip away from me, and I don't think of them again till we get the call with the news. When the tears begin to sting my eyes, I can't help but wonder: Was your goodbye supposed to be a blessing? Or is this forever my burden to carry? I can't shake the feeling that my curse is not in the dreaming but in the knowing, in the realization that every assurance can become an omen. I fear I'll live my whole life doomed to see the end coming, praying this time it won't lead to my undoing.

PANACEA

(n.) a remedy for all ills or difficulties

———

WHEN YOU'RE ADMITTED to the hospital, a casserole dish of lasagna appears at our door. I dig into it greedily, hoping that if I can fill those empty spaces inside of me with noodles and cheese and meat, maybe there won't be room for all the anxiety that has taken root inside of my gut. For days, I pick the burnt sauce from the edges of the pan, dreading the evening I'll finally lick its ceramic surface clean.

When you return home, too weak to walk into the house on your own, we find another lasagna waiting on the porch. Once you're secure in your bed, you cannot find the will to leave it, so I ladle my food onto a plate and settle into the seat at the dining room table that faces your bedroom door. I wonder if you're somewhere on the other side, picking at the long, flat noodles with your fork, if you even have the strength to sit up when you swallow. I imagine that when I take a bite, you do, too.

Another lasagna arrives in time for the chemo, which is good because standing beside the stove in the kitchen becomes an Olympian task that leaves you breathless for days. I have grown masterful in cutting out slices from the pan, and this precision is the only thing that keeps the structure of this house from caving in completely. I place one perfect square in the very center of a plate and take it to where you are recovering on the loveseat.

It begins to seem like every time one casserole dish is emptied, another appears full, like an impressive act of sorcery. "I never want to see another lasagna again," I overhear you say one night, but when another inevitably arrives at our doorstep, you spoon out a serving for yourself diligently, almost reverently, and eat every bite till it's gone.

PANOPLY

(n.) a magnificent or impressive array

————

I KNOCK ON THE DOOR of the villa; you answer with a smile. We do not share a history or a language, but your goodwill has invited me into your family home because if we do have anything in common, it's that we cannot come upon a stray without offering them a place to stay. In this land where I know no one, you have become a safe place.

While the rest of your family sets up tables on the lawn, you show me around the house, lingering in the living room, though I'm unsure if it's because you've noticed the falter in my step or if there's something you're desperate for me to see. You urge me forward with a reassuring smile, giving me permission to step fully into the room and look closer at what has caught my eye.

I'm not sure I've ever seen so much of everything all crammed into a twelve-square-foot room. On every available surface is something, it just takes me a moment to understand what. One table in the very center of the room holds nothing but globes—dozens of them, all different sizes and shapes and colors, as if they've been collected from every corner of the Earth. A cabinet beside the couch holds so many picture frames that it's almost impossible to see the photos within them, though I'm positive they all hold someone meaningful to you. And in every corner of the room, there are electric fans—old ones with chipping veneers, new ones painted in fluorescent shades, some that look too impractical to even work. Trying to understand everything sitting before me feels like standing in front of a pile of strangely shaped puzzle pieces that won't fit together.

I wind through the cleared paths between each exhibit, trying to soak in as much as I can while you wait patiently from the threshold. When I stop in front of one of the larger globes, you step forward to join me, reaching out to slowly revolve the sphere until we're facing North America. I smile and point to the very heart of the United States. "Home," I tell you.

You nod, then twist the globe until we're staring down at where we both stand now. Without speaking a word, I know your eyes are tracing my trek across the world.

We're interrupted by a burst of laughter from out on the lawn, and you smile and beckon me to follow you out. It's a shame, I can't help but think—I know I could spend hours in this curated museum of a room and continue to find something new hidden in every minute, but my time has already run out.

I wish I knew what all of this said about you. I wish I knew how to ask. These pieces of you have given me an insight you cannot otherwise convey to me—something I may never be able to put into words because the language between us is one no one else will ever be able to speak. Even if I never fully understand it, even if I never learn to translate it for anyone else, here in this room, I have learned something important about you—and in turn, it has become important to me.

PARAMNESIA

(n.) a disorder of memory, especially déjà vu

———

I STILL DREAM of you sometimes, and I don't understand how I remember you better when I'm asleep than I ever do awake.

PELAGIC

(adj.) relating to the open sea

———————

I'M STRETCHED OUT on the beach chair, letting the sun shower me in its drowsy summer rays when your shadow casts over me. I squint up at your glowing outline. "What?"

"You'll never guess what I just got us," you say with a mischievous slant to your smile, kicking up sand at me with your bare foot.

I brush the grains off my leg, frowning. I know you're right, I'll never guess because I cannot seem to comprehend the pathways of your brain, the way they twist and turn away from me. You are as unknowable as the farthest depths of the sea.

You seem to understand I've already given up on this game of yours because you're quick to give me the answer: "I convinced the lady at the marina to rent us a boat for free."

I almost laugh because there has never been a

sentence spoken that has encapsulated you so specifically. Instead, I lean back patiently and ask, "And how did you manage that?"

You meet the arch of my eyebrows with a wag of your own. "I've got my ways."

In this way, though, you're less mysterious than you think you are. I've seen the way the world bends to your will with just a bat of your eyelashes, how the atmosphere around you seems to change its shape to accommodate the mold of you; and though I'd never admit it, least of all to you, I've felt myself do it, too. So when I ask, "Do you even know how to drive a boat?" and you answer by stretching your hand toward me, I find myself taking it anyway.

Down near the water, I let you help me onto the boat, don't even complain when it rocks so violently I worry it might capsize before we even make it a full five feet away. When we're so far out that the beach starts to look like just a grainy scrap of fabric in the distance, you finally stop and let the waves rock us back and forth.

"Now what?" I ask you.

"Now we enjoy ourselves," you reply, stretching out like a cat who needs every fold of skin to find the sunlight.

I wonder what it's like to be you, to convince the world to give you a boat just because you can, to take it out into the water just to sit there in it, simply on a whim. To live your life in pursuit of just living your life, because the scariest thing to me seems to be the idea of purposelessness. You exist in the world so effortlessly that I sometimes envy you.

I'm so lost in my thoughts that I'm startled when you sit up suddenly, leaning over the side of the boat. "Oh my god, look!"

I turn quickly, reflexively, and wonder if I've already missed it. It takes me a moment to see what you do because, from where I stand, it just looks like miles of ocean in nearly all directions. But then I notice the outline of something forming, and when my eyes adjust, I wonder how I ever overlooked it in the first place. Below the boat are layers upon layers of translucent jellyfish floating past us, enough that it feels as though the whole sea is filled to the brim with them.

I clutch the edges of the boat beside you, leaning dangerously close to the surface of the water, trying to understand the pattern of their movement. "Where do you think they're going?" I ask you.

You shoot me an amused look. "Why do they need to have a destination?"

Once again, I don't have a guess for you, but this time I know you won't cut in with an answer. Instead, I stare down into the cloudy depths of the water, watching the jellyfish float away toward a destiny that I know, deep down, will always be a mystery to me.

PENITENCE

(n.) sorrow for sins or faults

———

I'M SORRY I RAISED my voice again, let me lower it to a whisper. I'm sorry I was hurt when you canceled plans, I'll try to be more flexible. I'm sorry that joke made you angry, I swear you'll never hear it again. I'm sorry I put away the dishes wrong, let me rearrange the whole cabinet. I'm sorry I forgot to turn off the light, I'll keep the house dark tomorrow. I'm sorry I texted three times in a row, I should've waited for your answer. I'm sorry I got mad when you called me crazy, I'm always too sensitive. I'm sorry I spent the whole night arguing, I'm no good at giving in. I'm sorry I can be so much sometimes, I wish I were easier. I'm sorry I couldn't make you happy—I couldn't do it for myself, either.

PENUMBRA

(n.) the shadow cast by light through an opaque object

————

YOU'RE BUTTONING UP your shirt, getting ready for the party, but you still haven't invited me. It wouldn't bother me so much if I hadn't heard you on the phone with some of your friends—some of mine, too—asking if anyone would accompany you. You pass by where I'm sitting at the kitchen table, pretending I don't notice.

I'm not sure when I became something so easily ignored. I used to be a wildfire, the spark of my emotions blinding, but now all that's left are the ashes we sweep under the rug. I've burnt myself out trying to become the kind of woman who doesn't need anything from you, who never asks for more than what you willingly give. In my quest to take up as little of your space as necessary, I've become translucent.

Don't you see me sitting here? I want to scream the question from across the room, but I fear I've become too fragile for the answer. Sometimes I'm convinced I wouldn't even know I was real if I couldn't see my shadow trailing one step behind me, silently assuring me, "You were here." I never recognized how badly I wanted to be seen until you looked right through me.

PEREGRINATION

(n.) a meandering journey

————

IT HAS TAKEN me years to get to this point, to be able to look you straight in the eye and—without letting my gaze float elsewhere, without hiding it under a joke or a hypothetical or an apology—say: This is who I am. It may not be what you hoped for, but this is the rawest part of me. You do not have to love it. You do not have to want it. You can choose to break the eye contact, can turn away completely, but that doesn't alter what I have finally found the courage to show you. This is who I am, and you can take it, accept it, offer me all the love you have to give anyway, or you can leave it behind—but you cannot and will not ever change it. I no longer have it in my heart to be anything else.

PETRICHOR

(n.) a distinctive, earthy, usually pleasant
odor that is associated with rainfall especially
when following a warm, dry period

———

WE STARE OUT the window of the little
Vietnamese restaurant on the corner downtown,
watching the raindrops pelt toward the ground like
a tsunami come to destroy the drought. "Well, fuck,"
you mutter under your breath, tracing the rim of
your mug absentmindedly with your forefinger.

We parked a few streets away, but you're running
late and the waitress is watching us wearily, waiting
for us to take our leave. You shoot me a look of an-
noyance and say, "Well, here goes nothing."

In the blink of an eye, you're gone. You push out of
your chair and out the door and out into the rain,
and I trail behind you, drenched the second I step
out onto the sidewalk.

We run, aggravated and sopping wet, but then you
stop at the street corner and look back at me for

a split second, your dark hair shimmering wet as it sticks in strands to your flushed cheeks. There's something about the exasperation in your eyes paired with your drowned puppy appearance that feels so strangely bizarre, and I can't stop the bubbles of laughter as they rise from my chest, inspired and unexpected. I am a woman possessed, unsure of what has taken hold of me, but your look of confusion only lasts for a second before you burst into giggles, too. And then we're both laughing hard as we dodge cars and slip into the back alley, splashing through puddles so deep they envelop our ankles and make us cry out in surprise.

We get to your car, shivering in drenched clothing that we wring out with shaking hands, still bent over in laughter. And it resonates with me so deeply that this simple moment is the first time in months our happiness isn't something we have to force.

PHANTASM

(n.) ghost

———

HALLOWEEN CAME and went, but your memory didn't come to haunt me this year. It didn't knock on my door, didn't ask to cross the threshold, didn't make its bed somewhere between my heart and my gut. I forgot to even expect it.

It took longer than anticipated, but I guess they were right when they said all wounds heal eventually—I grew so used to bleeding that I hardly noticed when I stopped. Maybe strength has less to do with willpower and more to do with the patience to let pain run its course—once it was gone, there was nothing left to prove you were ever here at all.

I know I learned something from you, but I can't remember what. The lessons are coded in my DNA now, stored away for another time, another place. Maybe that's what you meant when you said "forever" because I can't remember your voice or how you looked when the sunlight hit your face, but I'll always carry that part of you with me—those warning signs, that red tape, every bad gut feeling that convinces me to turn away. It's only when the storybook closes that you remember every happily ever after was once a cautionary tale.

All those years I spent breaking for you, only to forget the reasons why. There was something there once, something real, but it's all just a ghost story now.

PHOSPHENE

(n.) an impression of light that occurs
without light entering the eye

————

I'LL NEVER UNDERSTAND how these nights turn into mornings before our very eyes. I don't know where we find the words to fill every page of every hour like a diary for two, but you tell me about your father and your favorite pet and your first heartbreak as your windowpane glows with sleepy sunrays. I don't want to leave yet, don't want to enter the sundrenched reality that lays just beyond your bedroom door, but maybe if we close our eyes for a little while longer, we can pretend we've defied the laws of time, rewound the hours just to play them again, and the red burning behind our eyelids is nothing but your alarm clock illuminating into the dusk.

PHOSPHORESCENCE

(n.) an enduring luminescence
without sensible heat

————

SOMETIMES LIFE FEELS too heavy, like the sky is pressing down on my shoulders, constricting every corridor my lungs require to breathe. The world is big, but my anxiety is claustrophobic, and all I can do is curl up into a ball, smaller, smaller, hoping that the walls will stop moving in toward me, hoping that maybe by keeping still, the darkness might pass me by completely.

But then I hear it, those whispers from other rooms. There is someone in the kitchen making me coffee, humming thoughtlessly along with the machine. And there is the trill of the doorbell telling me there's a package outside my door, a gift from a friend who lives too far away. And there's the buzz of a text on my phone from someone I haven't heard from in years, but their words are soft, sweet. And there is my best friend leaning into the doorway, laughing at a joke I cannot hear, telling me to open the window, to let the world peek in.

As the sun filters in through the trees, warming the glass, I'm suddenly grateful for these shimmering fragments, these splinters of hope. I may never escape the shadows completely, but I will never stop pushing back the curtains to welcome in these iridescent moments of light.

PLUVIOPHILE

(n.) a lover of rain

————

YOU COME OVER to my apartment in the midst of the storm, huddle under the awning and knock on my door. I watch through the picture window as you wait, shivering, for me to let you in.

My friends all think you're good for me, that you might be my reprieve from the whirlwind relationships I'm used to. For me, love has always been tragedy, but you treat it like a home, someplace safe and warm, a shelter from the storm. Sometimes I'm afraid I'm not able to exist in such an environment. Because what if I am the rain? What if I bring the floods? Half the time I feel like an earthquake not yet realized, on the precipice of disaster. I fear I may be a threat to your very foundation.

On some days, I find myself thinking that maybe I can control it. Perhaps I can stop the hurricane with my bare hands, fill your cup with whatever I can gather in my palms. I can suppress the thunder, can redirect the hail. Who needs blizzards when I can offer you flurries that fleck the sky like glitter? If I try hard enough, I swear I can find the beauty in this chaos.

But if I'm being honest, I am tired. To love you would be to go against my very nature, to push against the forces of who I've always been. In a past life, I would have deconstructed my very being just to build the dams, but I cannot be that person anymore. I may be destruction, but I am also rebirth. I am resilience. I am rapture. I will demolish the life you've known, and together, we'll rebuild.

The truth is, I wasn't constructed to be the safe house you want me to be. I can only hope that some-day you'll learn to love the rain.

PROPINQUITY

(n.) nearness in place or time

———

SOMETIMES I THINK about how, before we met, we must've crossed paths a hundred times. How the park where I would search for fairies was the one where you would follow foxes through the trees. How our parents used to take us to the same summer fair in that little historical square, and how we spent all our weekends stealing popcorn at the same movie theater, and how you drove by my school every day on your way home. I think about how we once lived four floors apart in the same building, then four buildings apart on the same street, then four streets apart in the same town. How many times did we lock eyes and never realize? How many times did our strings of fate intertwine? Maybe that's why I've never been able to resist the pull—our lifetimes have been woven together, every moment so insignificant to the tapestry of its whole.

PYRRHIC

(adj.) achieved at excessive cost

———

I NEED YOU to know this: I won.

After years of this back and forth, this cat and mouse game where we playact both the predator and the prey, I have caught you in the cage of my teeth. I scratched your name out of every record, left your side of our pictures on the cutting room floor, let every bad memory burn through anything left of the good. I let my fury fan the flames, watched them scorch every inch of our earth. It didn't matter to me that I left behind every bridge we built to go up in smoke because, from the safe distance of my side of the story, I have made myself untouchable, unreachable, unblameable.

And I don't care if we never speak. I don't care if you spend the rest of your life wishing you never met me. If you wanted me to be the bigger person, you shouldn't have spent so many years letting me starve. Now I'll make a victory feast of the words I once threw at you because even the faint taste of regret can't taint the sweetness of this success.

I won, and now there's no proof left that we were ever happy at all.

QUIETUS

(n.) removal from activity; death

———

YOU CAN'T BRING yourself to tell me you don't think this is working out, so instead you say, "I'm going to bed early."

I don't have it in me to admit you're breaking my heart, so I tell you, "Maybe I'll call you tomorrow."

And you won't tell me you're falling in love with her, but you do mention you're going to see her again on Friday, which somehow seems crueler. I can only respond by averting my eyes from yours because withholding my attention feels like wielding a weapon, and the way you seek out my line of sight makes me feel like maybe I'm not the only one here with something to lose. But the longer I look away, the more I resent that moment when there's nowhere else to look but back at you. When our gazes collide, you don't ask me what's wrong, and I hate you for denying me the chance to deny you the truth.

Maybe it doesn't matter that what we really mean is always left hidden in the spaces punctuating our sentences, because the silence ringing between our phones says more than either of us has the words to admit. I'd rather rip the vocal cords from my throat than confess that we're still holding on to the pipe-dream of what we used to be. Maybe I'll never know how we went from so many endless nights of telling each other everything to all these empty mornings of saying nothing at all.

QUINTESSENCE

(n.) the most typical example or representative

———

ON THE FIRST spring day, when the sun stays out long enough to warm our winter-worn skin, we meet up for a walk at the park that winds between the train tracks and the creek. I tell you I've decided I want to build a garden—an impulsive decision I made only a week ago, mostly to prove to myself I can convince something to grow. You indulge my visions of plump tomatoes, of lettuce so fresh I can pluck it straight from the ground and rip into it with my teeth. My need for creation has found a new avenue, and now my imagination is insatiable. If you doubt my ability—which I suspect you do—you don't let it show.

You stop me mid-sentence when you see something along the side of the path, your attention wavering toward the cluster of green sprouting from the ground. I forget what I'm saying completely when you kneel beside it and tug at its roots until a clump comes untethered from the earth.

"I think it's a spring onion," you tell me, as if in explanation, then sniff the bit of skin that came in contact with the greenery. "Definitely smells like it."

You hold your hand toward me, just close enough that I catch a whiff of the bitter aroma and realize you're right—it reminds me of chopping vegetables in the kitchen on a bright afternoon. For a moment, I can almost imagine sinking a knife into its surface, the crisp sound of the blade cutting through.

"I can't believe you noticed that," I say, impressed. "Maybe you should be the one teaching me how to garden."

You scrunch your nose, rise back onto your feet. "Not sure about that," you reply as you begin to walk again. "I'm better at identifying something than getting it to grow."

Before I can even move to follow you, I'm struck by a realization: You have unintentionally identified what has always compelled me toward you, this strange ability of yours. Where I am the person who likes to play God, you are the one who notices what no one else does, who finds what's been there all along and tries to understand it. You see the world for what it really is and then choose to let it be. You would never try to force something to change, would never ask it to become anything more than it already is—not an onion, not yourself, not even me.

QUIXOTIC

(adj.) foolishly impractical especially
in the pursuit of ideals

———

IN MY MOST hopeful moments, I swear this
could still turn out the way it was always supposed
to. I could move to that city on the coast, into that
dingy little apartment you kept open in a tab on
your laptop for weeks. We could apply to those jobs
we always said we wanted, and even when the rejec-
tion letters pile up, we could shrug and try again.
We could travel across the world instead of always
saying "someday," instead of treating every plan like
we have one foot out the door. Maybe this time I'd
learn to say what I really mean, and maybe you'd
learn to open up instead of starting to resent me;
maybe this time I'd let go of my useless pride and
finally just apologize, the way I imagine doing when
I lie awake at night. Just give me the chance and I
know I could find a way to make this work—and
we'd be happy, we'd be happy, we'd be happy.

QUOTIDIAN

(adj.) commonplace, ordinary

———

I'M NOT SURE when happiness became making dinner together and eating on the living room floor, but I've started dreaming of grocery stores and long afternoon walks, of Saturday morning movies and coffeepots. Nothing says "I love you" quite like your hands wrapped around a mug of tea you made just because, just for me. I'll make freshly squeezed lemonade on the weekends, and I'll write in the early morning dawn when I'm too awake to sleep in, and on those late nights when we don't have anywhere to go, I want to dance around the kitchen in the golden microwave glow. I want to sew up the holes in your oldest sweatshirts, and I want to surprise you by baking all your favorite desserts, and when the springtime sun starts to warm the windows, I'll plant a garden on the balcony and watch the seeds till they grow. One day you'll ask why I can't stop smiling, but I won't know how to explain it—this laundry day yearning, this picket fence bliss.

RANTIPOLE

(n.) a wild reckless sometimes quarrelsome person

———

YOU'LL FIND US in midnight alleyways, glowing under flickering neon signs. We are champagne breath and smoky eyes, lipstick stains on compulsive lies. We are sweat-soaked dancers in dark corner bars where half-dressed half-humans whisper empty promises into deaf ears. We are frantic billiard balls turning in cacophonous rhythms, colliding full force and dispersing within minutes. We are low beats on broken drums, guttural groans that reverberate through sticky walls and stained floors that reek of cigarette butts and bile. We are secret glances and stolen kisses and elation, exhilaration, exultation. We are the agonies and ecstasies, the woes and wonders of being young and uninhibited and alive.

REDOLENT

(adj.) full of a specified fragrance;
evocative, suggestive

———

IT'S MY LAST DAY in town, and we've both grown too used to saying goodbye, so instead you say, "Let's go to the lavender fields." I have a half-empty suitcase waiting for me somewhere in the apartment I will soon no longer call home, but I'd rather miss my flight than miss this last moment with you, so I shrug and say, "Okay."

As you drive, both of us hum along to the radio, but when we reach the gravel road to the farm and see the gate is locked, my jaw clenches shut. I don't completely understand why I'm so devastated by this small, cruel twist of fate, but when you look at me, I know you feel it, too.

"It's okay," I assure you. "Maybe we'll come back another day."

It's wishful thinking, but I suppose, at this point, it all sort of is. We know this day will end in an ellipsis because this period of time is marked by uncertainty and we aren't sure who we'll be when we get to the other side. Every promise now begins to feel like a plea: Please don't forget about this. Please come back to me.

But these maybes are not enough for you, not anymore, not when we've already come this far. "Come on," you say, beckoning me to follow you out of the car. It isn't until we're standing in front of the iron gate that I realize what you want from me.

"But I'm wearing a skirt," I protest weakly. "And heels."

And finally, there it is: that mischievous smile, that tilt of your head. "As if that's ever stopped you before."

I roll my eyes, and just like that, the heaviness is gone and we're us again: you, who will never let an obstacle keep you out; me, who will never let my own bad choices stop me from making another. It's who we've always been, but more importantly, it's who we've always been to each other, and I know the unruliness that lives inside me is in part because I knew you.

So with the support of your shoulder, I climb up the

gate and hoist myself over. When it's your turn to follow, I offer you my hand, and you grip it like a lifeline. When we've both made it to the other side unscathed, I dust myself off and look around at the overgrown grass and ask, "Well, now what?"

I know I'll never forget the way you laugh when you reply, "How am I supposed to know?" Neither of us has any idea what we're looking for here—maybe there's nothing to find. Maybe there's just us, standing side-by-side, your fingers against the back of my hand, the smell of lavender thick and sweet in the air. Maybe we will find a piece of this moment in a million other places—a department store perfume, a stranger's voice, the warmth of someone else's skin—and when we close our eyes, it will bring us back to each other. Even though I still don't know how to tell you goodbye, I think these maybes could be enough for me.

RESIDUUM

(n.) something residual

———

WHEN I STEP on the needle that goes straight through my foot, you carry me to the kitchen. You set me down on a wooden stool and work the metal out of my skin carefully, never flinching as I whimper into the alcove between your shoulder and neck. "It's out now," you tell me, but I can't stop crying. "Where does it hurt?" you ask me, but I couldn't say. The pinpoint of pain may be gone but the ache is always there, always festering, long after I've forgotten the reason why.

RESPLENDENT

(adj.) shining brilliantly

————

THE REVERBERATION OF the trumpets snake through these humid New Orleans roads, but the sound recoils when it reaches us, daunted by the crescendo of your voice. We're fighting about something, though in our drunken haze, it's hard for me to understand what—all I know is I'm trying to suffocate the flames of your anger, but all it's really doing is suffocating me. You can't stand to look at me, and I'm not sure what else to do, so I spend the rest of the night trailing ten steps behind you, just a shadow on the blacktop of Bourbon Street.

We end up at a karaoke bar, the kind of place where any other night we'd laugh and dance to the music, but in this parallel universe, you dissipate into the crowd, leaving me to haunt the edges of the room. I want so badly for you to look my way, to notice me just once, just for now, but when I finally catch a glimpse of you, I watch you watch the stage, spellbound.

I hate how it always seems to end like this, how I have to beg for these scraps of your attention when all I've ever craved was the warmth of your limelight. I hate how I could be everything and still be nothing you want, because I've tried and tried and tried and it's never been enough. I hate that I've started to wonder if this is all that's meant for me.

I'm so busy looking at you that I don't notice the MC is onstage looking at me, crooking his finger in my direction as the music starts to play. Someone tugs my arm and says, "It's you, it's you," and the crowd that became your camouflage is suddenly the undercurrent that pushes me forward, right toward the hand that pulls me onto the stage. When the MC hands me a microphone, I take it; when he looks at me expectantly, I let the first shaky lyrics leave my lips. It's only when the crowd starts cheering that the sound of the city comes to life in front of me, its electricity the shock that brings me back into my body. Under the spotlight, in front of a hundred people I'll never know, I'm finally the one who's shining, and for the first time all night, I don't even care that you might be somewhere out there watching me, too.

RUTILANT

(adj.) having a reddish glow

———

THE WILDFIRE OF the sunset burns bright from the windows behind me, so blinding in its reddish hues that I can't look at it for more than a few seconds at a time. Instead, I watch the way the light seeps golden onto the linoleum floor, electrifying the world under my feet.

"Have you ever been in a moment where it feels like a crime that you don't have a camera?"

I start at the sound of your voice and look up to see you standing across from me. You're holding your hands out in front of you, forming your fingers into a rectangle—forefinger to thumb, forefinger to thumb—and squinting at me from between them as if watching through a screen.

I shift uncomfortably, feeling the golden light mold to my movements from behind. I open my mouth, the taste of sarcasm already coating my tongue, but I cannot find the words to fill it. The quirk of your lips is all I need to know I've been caught, but I refuse to let you believe I am so easily affected, so I recover by raising a skeptical brow. "I don't know," I say, hoping you can't see past my feigned nonchalance. "I don't take a lot of pictures."

It's true—I've always been a writer, not an artist; the world of words makes more sense to me, at least when I'm not the subject in your viewfinder. But you grin like you've been let in on a secret, your arms falling into a shrug. "You'd get it if you could see yourself from here," you assure me. "You're glowing."

SACCHARINE

(adj.) overly or sickishly sweet

———

I DON'T KNOW what I'm supposed to do with all these memories you left behind. They are sugar-coated photographs I leave hanging in these empty rooms, quiet reminders that you were once here, that even though you packed away everything else into boxes and moved them into someone else's home, and even though I wake up every day to the proof that you left me here alone, you once filled every vacant space surrounding me with light.

SANGUINE

(adj.) marked by eager hopefulness

———

THE CLOUDS LOOM over us, thick and angry, but since I only have a few hours left till my flight leaves, you take me to your favorite beach. "You're not allowed to visit me without coming here," you tell me. "The weather can wait."

The storm seems to agree with you, creeping along the edges of the horizon but never quite reaching us as we walk along the shore. When the water washes over our feet, you point down to show me how the sand glimmers like gold, leaving flecks of glitter along our skin. I'm fascinated by this trace of magic we have uncovered on an otherwise dreary day.

"I could stay here forever," I say as I dip my hand into the waves, watching as it reemerges with a Swarovski sheen. Right now, it's true. Even though the sky is threatening to drown us out any minute, I'd take the downpour over the everyday drudgery that awaits me the second the plane touches down back home. I have already grown sick of the landlocked feeling that has come with adult-hood, as if my newfound freedom has come with a stipulation: You now have the ability to do what you want, but rarely the resources—the time, the money, the energy, the curiosity. Life has become less shiny in the past few years, but standing in this shimmering ocean makes me feel an inkling of the wonder that escaped me once the door to my childhood slammed shut.

As we head further down the beach, I notice some-thing drifting in the water. "Look!" I say, pointing toward it.

"What is it?" you ask.

I can't tell from where I stand, but I'm drawn by the way the sun makes its surface glow. I wade out into the water, unconcerned by your protests or the bite of winter in the waves drenching my skirt. When I grow closer, I realize this unidentified floating object is a single yellow rose.

I rush back to your side, holding the rose over my head until I am close enough to hand you this aquatic offering; you take it with a grateful smile and shake the sea from its petals. "You're crazy," you say, the words blanketed in adoration.

We continue our stroll but stop again when we notice two more orbs of yellow surfing in on the tide. I collect the flowers and we distribute them between us, only to find three more farther up the beach.

"This is so bizarre," you tell me, perplexed. "I've never seen anything like this the whole time I've lived here."

"Where could they have come from?" I ask, wringing the water from the hem of my clothes, but you don't have any theory to offer that's any more compelling than my own.

By the time we head back to the car, we have found a whole bouquet of golden roses washed up in the ocean, which we lay across the dashboard for the rest of the drive to the airport. I can't stop looking at them, amazed by this strange turn of events.

"I know it sounds crazy, but this feels like a sign," I say, reaching out to touch the petals carefully. "Like a gift from the universe."

Without taking your eyes from the road, you smile. "It's funny. I was just thinking the same thing."

When we say goodbye, hugging in the drop-off lane outside the terminal, you tuck one single rose into the pocket of my backpack. "As a reminder," you tell me, seeming to understand no other explanation is necessary. Before I disappear through the doors, I glance up at the sky one last time and realize the storm has overlooked us completely.

SAUDADE

(n.) deep longing or nostalgia for
something that no longer exists

————

SOMETIMES I DRIVE past your favorite bar
and I see it from the corner of my eye so suddenly
I have to do a double-take: you and me, twirling to-
gether on the patio, laughing with our heads thrown
back. No matter how many times it happens, I'm
never ready for the way we smudge across my vision,
prickling at the back of my eyelids. I always have to
look away before I'm blinded.

But god, you made me illuminate with a light I'm
not even sure I have anymore. I remember the af-
ternoon we danced on tabletops, and I remember
the night we stayed awake to whisper our darkest
secrets into four o'clock rooms, and I remember
when we jumped into the fountain in the middle of
the road, fully clothed, ignoring every car that leered
in our direction. We filled up all the spaces others
had left empty with so much of everything, of each
other, so that we never had to feel alone. With you,
I never had to know what it meant to be on my own.

But we aren't like that anymore. You never call. And when your favorite songs play on the radio now, I only hear the ghosts of your laughter from the passenger seat; and all those inside jokes become a dead language that only I speak, the slow decay of my mother tongue; and everyone I meet who shares your name becomes just another person doomed to disappoint me, reminding me that even when you're not here, you somehow always are. It seems so useless now that I've memorized every curve of every road that leads to your house, but even though I'll never see them again, I'll always miss those nights when they opened up in front of me, their concrete currents carrying me to you. I'm not sure I'll ever know how to face the fact that nothing makes me lonelier than all these things I once considered home.

SCINTILLA

(n.) spark, trace

———

WE DON'T RUN into each other often anymore, but sometimes when we do, I see it in your eyes: this flash of recognition, as if, for a minute, you're not looking at what the years have made me but at who I was when you knew me. This glimmer of hope that maybe, after all this time, there's a chance I still could be her. It's always gone by the time we say goodbye.

SEMPITERNAL

(adj.) of never-ending duration

———

WE'RE SITTING ACROSS from one another at the little bar table, letting the gin and tonics loosen our lips. It's easy to open up when the lights are half-dimmed and our brains are half-functioning; for once, I don't feel like I constantly have to edit what I want to say before I let myself say it, and in that way, maybe I'm more myself than I've ever been.

"I'm scared no one will love me the way I am," you whisper across the table, a confession that feels almost funny to me because here I am, looking to you, loving you for every piece you've ever shown me. But I know you aren't looking for a contradiction, just an acknowledgment of the way you feel; I know what it's like to want your fears to simply be heard.

"Sometimes I worry nothing I do matters," I admit after a moment. "Like I could do everything I can to make a difference but none of it means anything."

We let our thoughts lay out on the table between us,

small offerings of friendship that seem to say: This is the softest part of me. I trust you to hold it gently.

You trace your forefinger across the tabletop absent-mindedly, disrupting the ring of water left behind from your empty glass, then look up at me deliberately. You lick your lips, take a breath. "You're always so worried that you won't change the world," you say slowly, "but you already have."

I almost laugh. Me, changed the world? Most of the time, I'm convinced I'm not even capable of changing my own life. I don't know when I started to feel this way, but these days the thought has started to solidify, pressing down against my throat. What if I never have anything to show from these years of my life? What if every pursuit comes up empty, no matter how hard I try? Every action I take has begun to feel like a scream into the void, a footprint quickly weathered away by the sands of time, and I'm terrified they will soon come to bury me, too.

You seem to read my mind through my expression, your mouth twitching into a frown. "Look at me," you say, suddenly resolute, and don't continue until you've finally caught my gaze with your own, holding on to it tightly. "You have changed the world," you tell me again. "I know because you've changed mine."

SERENDIPITY

(n.) a phenomenon of finding
valuable things not sought for

———————

"I'M SO LUCKY TO exist in this moment with you," you write to me in postscript like an existential "I love you."

I think about these words all the time now; they follow me everywhere I go. I grab a cup of coffee with my sister, and as we sift through her wedding photos, she tells me she's pregnant with her first child. I'm so lucky to exist in this moment with you. I laugh with my mother when the dog gallops through a snowbank so tall it almost swallows him whole. I'm so lucky to exist in this moment with you. I listen to a boy tell me stories of his father that he lost last June but who he's trying so hard to resurrect for me. I'm so lucky to exist in this moment with you. A stranger rear-ends my car but later writes me a message to say that meeting me was a happy accident. I'm so lucky to exist in this moment with you.

It's the simplest of things, yet somehow the most profound. Out of everywhere we could be in the universe, out of everyone we could be, we're here and now, you and me. I don't know if this is what they call fate or if we are just a series of coincidences, I just know that this means everything to me, even if it means nothing to anyone else. If this is all just an accident, it's the happiest one of all.

SILLAGE

(n.) perfume scent that lingers after someone leaves

———

MISSING YOU IS more than the feeling that something is gone—it's the resurrection of every-thing you had been. It's walking through crowds and smelling your cologne on foreign bodies. It's hear-ing your words on someone else's lips. It's seeing someone smile and feeling that pang of recognition because your eyes used to light up in all the same ways and it makes me wish I were looking at you. You are the man buying coffee in the shop next door, and you are my neighbor playing his guitar on the front porch, and you are every damn person I've walked by today, but I try my best not to let it show that I recognize you.

Missing you is the fear of falling asleep and seeing you in my dreams. Of waking up to another day of finding you in everything around me.

SOLIVAGANT

(n.) a solitary wanderer

———

THE SUN RISES behind the mountains as I sketch their shape onto the back of my plane ticket. I'm not ready to say goodbye to them yet, so I sit at the airport café next to the floor-to-ceiling windows, trying to memorize every swell and slope of the landscape.

Homesickness has always worked in the opposite direction for me. All I ever long for is the places I've had to leave. I have buried my heart in too many cities to count, and I'm not sure what that says about me. Does it make me less happy? Less whole? Will I always feel like something is missing?

All I know is that by the end of the day, I will fall asleep in my own bed and dream of lands I haven't seen in years. When I awake, I will drown in all my heartache. And someday, when I can no longer bear this pain in my chest, I will beg you to hook me up to an electrocardiogram so I can turn to the screen and once again watch the mountains come to life before me.

SOMNAMBULIST

(n.) person who sleepwalks

———

THERE'S SOMETHING about those days I find hard to remember, as if I'd been living in a haze, blinded by your splendor. I was ensnared by your charm, bewitched by your guise, and I could never eat, and I could never sleep, but I couldn't open my eyes. You were the Pied Piper playing my heartstrings like a melody, drowning out my senses and lulling me into your daydream. I followed every note like a sheep to the slaughter, let you lead me to the river and then deny me any water, and I know now you could have beaten me and broken me and I never would have cared. Half asleep or half alive, I would have followed you anywhere.

SONOROUS

(adj.) full or loud in sound

————

YOUR LAUGHTER pierces the silence and echoes through the rooms of your empty apartment. It fills me with something strong, that noise, and I'm not sure if it's because there's nothing more beautiful than the sounds you make or if there's nothing more beautiful than the knowledge that I was the one who made you make them.

SUPINE

(adj.) lying on the back or with the face upward

———

WE LIE ON THE cold, hard ground, huddled side-by-side in sleeping bags we found in the garage. The night is so clear we can see every line of the Milky Way spiraling above us, a stream of stars I dream of diving into, hoping those cosmic currents might take me away. In my hometown, the nights are only illuminated by the city lights, their glare blinding me from anything that might lay beyond them. Lying here, the whole universe has opened up before me, and with it, so has my narrow slice of the world.

You shiver beside me, bringing me back to Earth, at least for a moment. A coyote cries out in the distance and we both stop breathing; you wrap your hand around my arm tightly, but neither of us moves. Not yet.

"How long?" I whisper, my words drifting upwards in plumes of steam.

"Soon," you whisper back. "Just watch."

We stay there, limbs intertwined, frozen from the fear and the cold and the need to witness a miracle. We peel our eyes so wide open that they begin to burn; we resist the urge to blink the tears away, terrified that in those microseconds, we'll miss our chance completely.

Then we see it, streaked across the velvet sky: A shooting star.

"Make a wish!" you cry, your fingers digging into my arm. "Fast!"

I close my eyes tightly, trying to hold the magic of the moment in the knot of my fists. *I wish, I wish, I wish.*

I wish I were prettier. And I wish my mother's cancer were gone. I wish the world were a softer place, and I wish there were less darkness in my brain, and sometimes I wish I weren't here at all. I can't bear to waste all this want on the wrong thing, though, not when so little feels right anymore, so instead I wish for a sign—something, anything.

You elbow me in the side, breaking off my train of thought. When I open my eyes, the sky has been lit up, electrified. Meteors paint the darkness, the glimmer of their tails cascading toward the Earth like the whole stratosphere might collapse down upon us. It is terrifying. And it is exhilarating. And I know in this moment this is exactly how I want to live the rest of my life: bright-eyed and belly-up to the world.

"Don't be afraid to make another wish," you grin. "We have a sky full of them."

SYZYGY

(n.) the nearly straight-line configuration of
celestial bodies in a gravitational system

———

WE WERE ALWAYS so different, but despite the
warning signs, I wanted to believe we could coex-
ist. It never occurred to me that if one of us were
ever going to be happy, the other would have to be
eclipsed.

TENDER

(adj.) marked by, responding to, or
expressing the softer emotions

———

SHE TELLS ME I'm getting my softness back,
that she can see it in the way I write about you. It's
difficult to admit it's true, that after years of polish-
ing my shield and sharpening my sword, preparing
for the devastating voyage, I'm suddenly all silk and
gossamer. In your hands, I fall apart, unraveling like
the tapestry Penelope ripped to shreds every night
while she waited for her heart to find its way home.
Sometimes I worry that's the woman I'm becoming,
the kind who comes undone at the thought of losing
the velvet of your voice, the satin of your smile. It
seems fitting, even fated, that my reckoning isn't the
capsizing I've braced myself for but the whisper of
the waves lapping against my ankles, enticing me
to jump in.

TINTINNABULATION

(n.) the ringing or sounding of bells

————

WHEN I SCROLL through my contacts, my thumb still stutters over your name, mimicking the jolt of my heart in my throat. It's been ten years since I've heard from you, but I can't bring myself to delete your number, even though I know I'll never use it, even though I'm not sure it still belongs to you. Most days, I don't have it in me to admit this to anyone, but today, I will confess: Sometimes I pray my finger will slip, that I'll hit the wrong button and when I look down at the screen, I'll realize my phone is already calling you.

This time, I promise to let the airwaves find you. This time, I promise to let the line connect. This time, I promise to let the phone ring for as long as you'll allow it, even though I know, deep down, you'll be on the other side doing the same.

TRAVAIL

(n.) work especially of a painful or laborious nature

————

NO ONE EVER told me womanhood would feel like being punched in the gut over and over and over again, only to be told it's my fault for never learning to handle the pain.

UNMOORED

(adj.) no longer attached to a mooring

———

I'VE NEVER BEEN very good at directions, even in this city we've come to call home. I am always driving the wrong way or turning too soon or so discombobulated that I'm not even sure where to start. But for some reason, you seem to like it when I drive, always forgoing the wheel to navigate from the passenger seat. I never thought much of it, not really, not until that night when I asked which route to take and instead of saying something vague like, "You'll turn left eventually," you counted out the lanes on the road and said, "Stay in this third one, it'll take us where we want to go."

For a lost girl like me, there's nothing more intimate than these small ways you surprise me, how you seem to understand my brain in ways I'm not even sure I do. The way you pluck my words out of thin air when I can't seem to find them, how you can extract my emotions when they're too heavy to describe, how you remember every detail of every story I've told you long after I've forgotten them. How you seem to understand intuitively that I've never really grasped where I exist in relation to the rest of the world, not in any of the ways that matter, and so you do something as simple as showing me exactly where I belong. I have always felt untethered, always halfway gone to Neverland, but you hold me down with tender hands and help these unsteady feet find their way home.

VACILLATE

(v.) to waver in mind, will, or feeling

————

MY LOVE IS lunar—it comes in phases, shrinking to nothing, then growing full. Oscillating—waxing, waning—an endless cycle of caring less and wanting more.

VERKLEMPT

(adj.) overcome with emotion

———

THIS GRIEF HAS grown cosmic, though I try not to let it show. I want you to believe I am still vast enough to hold all this hurt, so I make myself celestial, my smile solar, if only so you won't notice the worst parts of me are gaining gravity and I am starting to lose control. If you could probe the crater of my ribcage, you'd find a black hole where my heart once lived, threatening to swallow me whole. I am a solar system of atoms ready to implode, and when it all comes collapsing in on me, you'll watch from afar and wonder how something that once shone so brightly could be extinguished so completely. But even supernovas are so blinding we sometimes forget they're dying, and in these flashes of brilliance, so is a part of me.

VERTIGO

(n.) a sensation of whirling motion; dizziness

———

HALFWAY UP THE mountain, you ask if we can stop the car, and I agree because the shading of your face can't amount to anything good. The rain has gotten stronger and the roads narrower as we ascend toward the peak, so we pull over to the side of the road while you struggle to catch your breath.

"It's worse near the edge," you tell me when you find the balance to speak. "It wasn't so bad till I looked down."

It's not until we start winding back up the mountain that I make the mistake of looking out the window and understand what you mean. Up here, so close it feels like we could hold out our arms and touch the heavens, reality has become upturned, distorted. Below us is a dark quilt of clouds, the lightning flashing and flaring in the storm raging beneath our feet, while above us there is nothing but miles of rocky terrain looming over our heads like a shadow of the Earth. Instinctively, I reach out to grasp your hand, our fingers clasping together tightly, as if maybe we can hold each other into place just long enough to reach the top, where we pray to find the world right-side up again.

VESTIGIAL

*(adj.) remaining as the last small part
of something that existed before*

———

I SHATTER MYSELF into pieces and arrange
them on a silver platter to lay at your feet. You ex-
amine them one by one, turning each over in your
palms, then handpick your favorites and leave the
rest rotting on the hardwood floor. It doesn't mat-
ter that I can stand in a room full of mirrors and no
longer distinguish who I am from who you want me
to be—you've loved those pieces of me so beautifully
I've forgotten anyone could love me whole.

WHELVE

(v.) to cover or hide something

————

YOU HOLD ME in your arms like I am a swaddle of broken parts you're desperate to hold together. I can't remember the last time I let anyone treat me so tenderly, but I am too tired from holding up these walls to find the strength to push you away. I let your heat lull me into the false sense of security you always try to feed me, because I may not believe you, but I'd like to believe I could. I don't have it in my heart to trust you, but I'll let you rock me to sleep.

You look at me like I am a bird with broken wings. Your touch is hesitant, gentle, because you know one wrong move will make my whole universe cave in and it will swallow me whole. You know that once I'm gone, you won't be able to find me again. You're not sure if you're more afraid of losing me or realizing you've already lost me long ago.

So you follow my scars like they're a map to the answers, but they cannot lead you to all those secrets buried somewhere deep inside. They are locked inside the Pandora's box of my heart and I am too afraid to crack open the lid to ever let you in. I am full of chaos and catastrophes that threaten to tear our worlds apart.

But if you let me, I can pretend things are different. If you let me, I can pretend I'm almost whole. If you let me, I can bury myself in you so I can bury the hurt farther, farther, into depths unknown to the human heart, into places you cannot excavate until long after I'm gone.

WHIMSICAL

(adj.) lightly fanciful

———

WE GROW UP restless little creatures imprisoned in our homes, taught there's nothing good for us hidden in the woods. They tell us there are too many dangers twisted in the thorns, too many monsters waiting in the underbrush. They make us promise we'll stay away.

But then they turn their heads and there we go again, ducking under low branches and climbing over fallen trees. In this woodland wonderland, we are finally free. We rub our cheeks with the pinks of the petals, bleed the berries till they stain our lips, let the mud on our bare feet baptize us unto the earth and begin our metamorphosis. We know there is something out here, something more, so we collect stones in the chalice of our palms, christening them the runes of our protection, and lose ourselves on the path unknown. In our search for elves and fairies and dryads, for all the magic we'd been promised but never presented, we become the wild things written within the storybooks our parents read as we drift off to sleep.

And when we return to our mothers and fathers, crowns of twigs tangled in our hair, we listen to their lectures with a smile. Because they don't understand, but we do. We've found the worlds they lost when they grew up and stopped believing in fairytales.

WISTFUL

(adj.) full of yearning or desire
tinged with melancholy

———

IN THESE DWINDLING days of summer, we spend our afternoons stretched side-by-side on the dock, letting the sun melt away all the walls we have left between us. There is nothing we have to do, nowhere we need to be, so we pass the time playing a game we call "Someday, we will…" We venture out into the future together, never moving a muscle.

You're always the first to start: "Someday, we will open a bakery."

I'm always quick to follow: "Someday, we will go to Paris."

"Someday, we'll be each other's bridesmaids," you add.

"Someday, our kids will be best friends, too."

It all seems so clear from here, from this sixteenth summer on the dock in the middle of nowhere. It doesn't even cross our minds that neither of us will ever make it to France, let alone with each other. We'll never open a bakery, but every time I make your favorite kind of cookies, I'll think of you. Instead of standing beside you on your wedding day, I'll hear you got married from a friend of a friend, and when I ask, "To who?" they'll say, "Oh, I don't know, some guy," and it'll hit me that for the first time in my entire life, I won't know your full name.

Someday, we will delete all the photos of each other off our phones to make room for other people. Someday, our birthdays will become just another empty space on the calendar, a mundane Tuesday afternoon. Someday, we'll go weeks, even months, without crossing each other's minds, but today I can't imagine lasting a day without speaking to you, so I'll take these empty words for granted, never fully understanding the weight of this moment until it's already long gone.

WOEBEGONE

(adj.) exhibiting great woe, sorrow, or misery

———

WHEN THE SKY closes up and sinks into a cold, harsh gray, spitting rain against the windowpanes, I lock all the doors and draw the curtains, take refuge under as many blankets as I can. When the world outside is dying, how can anyone feel alive? I pretend to hibernate through the day, eyes wide open.

The dreariness permeates my skin and settles in my bones, pooling inside the marrow. It is a part of me in ways I am not even a part of myself, yet an entity of its own, an interloper. Is it normal to feel both too full and so empty? I am somehow both the vessel and the furnishings, but I am also neither at all. I am a fluctuating existence. Do I own this sadness or does it own me?

And it's not the way it used to be, back when the hurt made a permanent home of me. I know the sun will come out eventually, evaporating this ache from me. But sometimes, in the shadow of my own happiness, I still feel that rain cloud hanging overhead, anticipating the downpour. Is it wrong of me to crave the storm? It is an old friend, a familiar lullaby, a reminder of the places I've been. I refuse to walk this path backward, but for a moment, I'll reminisce.

YEARNING

(n.) a tender or urgent longing

————

YOU'LL NEVER SEE the way my face mirrors the phone when your name lights up the screen. You will never know that I bite my lip when you speak, that I hide my smile from empty rooms as if it's a secret even blank walls might expose. I wonder if you hear the admiration in every "hello" or if it's just another detail you write off, another confirmation that you do not dissect my words the way I do yours. I collect the syllables in your sentences to repeat to myself on the rainy days when you forget to call.

These nights produce a magic I cannot seem to replicate. When I listen to you speak, the gap between us begins to diminish, and thousands of miles turn to hundreds, and hundreds into none, and the low hum of your voice fills the spaces next to me with warmth until I am no longer lying in bed alone. You always say goodbye first, unaware that my fingers hover above the "end call" button for moments afterward, lingering longingly, because each time the line cuts, I'm the one left bleeding, and that is a tragedy all of its own.

ZEPHYR

(n.) a gentle breeze

———————

WE SIT BY THE harbor, our sore legs stretched out before us as we breathe in the last of the summer air. I close my eyes and let the sun kiss my face and wonder if I'll ever find myself here again, thousands of miles from home in a land that looks so different from my own.

"Do you ever just wish you could stay here forever?" you ask. I do.

We don't speak as we watch a group of teenagers dance on the other side of the water. Their music floats toward us on the breeze, rustling through our hair and skimming the surface of our skin. It feels voyeuristic, almost, to gaze at them from afar. I can't tear my eyes away as they take turns diving headfirst into the harbor.

It's strange how I'm suddenly no longer in Copenhagen but instead on the shore of a lake in Missouri, watching myself at a different age. I'm singing at the top of my lungs while spinning on a wooden dock with my best friend, both of which I'll someday never see again. I'm jumping into the murky water, unafraid of anything that may lie in wait deep beneath it. I am young and naïve and happy. I am not that girl anymore, though—now I am the woman on the shore, watching wistfully, remembering exactly how it once felt to be someone else.

But then I'm back at the harbor, staring out at the water, a thousand versions of myself between now and the girl I was then. You look over at me and I wonder if you're lost somewhere in another time, too, thinking all the same things. Instead, you ask, "What if we never get this back?"

There are a million things we'll never get back, I want to tell you. We are a lifetime of losses. We shed ourselves like snakeskin over and over again. We leave parts of us behind.

Someone once told me that just because we lose something doesn't mean it didn't matter. Right now, we are basking in the breeze wafting off the water, remembering what it felt like to believe nothing would ever change. We are holding on to this moment tightly, grateful to exist in it and half-afraid it's about to be pried from our fingers. We are happy.

I know this now: It matters.

ACKNOWLEDGMENTS

The first thank yous belong to my first supporters—my parents—for always encouraging me to follow my dreams, even when the world told me they were unrealistic. I am who I am because you have loved me, and I hope I've made you proud.

The next thank yous are some of the most important because you could not hold this book in your hands if it weren't for the wonderful team that turned dream into reality: Chris, Noelle, KJ, Molly, Kelly, and everyone else on the Thought Catalog Books team.

The rest of my gratitude belongs to the people who have helped me shape this book throughout the years of its progress: Marissa, Curie, Hannah, Samantha, Annette, Kristin, Jared, Allison, Trisha, Tobi, Jackie, and Sydney. There were a lot of times I almost gave up, but this is proof that you have made an impact on my life—none of this would exist if not for you.

CALLIE BYRNES

is a writer from Kansas City. You can keep up with her work here:

INSTAGRAM

@wordsbycalliebyrnes

or @callie.byrnes

TWITTER

@calliebyrnes

TIKTOK

@callie.byrnes

THOUGHT CATALOG Books

Thought Catalog Books is a publishing imprint of Thought Catalog, a digital magazine for thoughtful storytelling, and is owned and operated by The Thought & Expression Co. Inc., an independent media group based in the United States of America. Founded in 2010, we are committed to helping people become better communicators and listeners to engender a more exciting, attentive, and imaginative world. The Thought Catalog Books imprint connects Thought Catalog's digital-native roots with our love of traditional book publishing. The books we publish are designed as beloved art pieces. We publish work we love. Pioneering an author-first and holistic approach to book publishing, Thought Catalog Books has created numerous best-selling print books, audiobooks, and eBooks that are being translated in over 30 languages.

ThoughtCatalog.com | **Thoughtful Storytelling**

ShopCatalog.com | **Shop Books + Curated Products**

MORE FROM
THOUGHT CATALOG BOOKS

A Gentle Reminder
—*Bianca Sparacino*

When You're Ready, This Is How You Heal
—*Brianna Wiest*

Everything You'll Ever Need
(You Can Find Within Yourself)
—*Charlotte Freeman*

Moments To Hold Close
—*Molly Burford*

Face Yourself. Look Within.
—*Adrian Michael*

**THOUGHT
CATALOG**
Books

THOUGHTCATALOG.COM